R2-00

SPIRIT OF ENGLAND

By the same author and published by Collins

The Story of England
MAKERS OF THE REALM B.C.–1272
THE AGE OF CHIVALRY 1272–1381
THE ELIZABETHAN DELIVERANCE
KING CHARLES II 1630–1685
RESTORATION ENGLAND 1660–1702

Samuel Pepys
THE MAN IN THE MAKING 1633–1669
THE YEARS OF THE PERIL 1669–1683
THE SAVIOUR OF THE NAVY 1683–1689
PEPYS AND THE REVOLUTION

The Napoleonic Wars
THE YEARS OF ENDURANCE 1793–1802
YEARS OF VICTORY 1802–1812
THE AGE OF ELEGANCE 1812–1822
NELSON
THE GREAT DUKE

ENGLISH SAGA 1840–1940

The Alanbrooke Diaries
THE TURN OF THE TIDE 1939–1943
TRIUMPH IN THE WEST 1943–1946

English Social History
THE MEDIEVAL FOUNDATION
PROTESTANT ISLAND
THE FIRE AND THE ROSE
THE LION AND THE UNICORN

JIMMY

JACKETS OF GREEN

A THOUSAND YEARS OF BRITISH MONARCHY

ARTHUR BRYANT

SPIRIT

OF

ENGLAND

COLLINS
St. James's Place, London
1982

William Collins Sons & Co. Ltd
London · Glasgow · Sydney · Auckland
Toronto · Johannesburg

Bryant, Arthur

Spirit of England
1. Great Britain—History
I. Title
942   DA30

ISBN 0-00-217084-1

First published 1982

© Arthur Bryant 1940, 1947, 1960, 1971
1978, 1980, 1982

Made and printed in Great Britain by
William Collins Sons & Co. Ltd., Glasgow

To
Wilfred House,
the dear friend
of my Oxford youth,
who in 1918,
an acting Brigade Major
of twenty-three,
held against odds
a vital gap in the British line
and so helped to halt the German
drive on the Channel ports

Contents

Introduction

This book is about two things: the spirit of England and the writing and teaching of history. It has been evoked by the valour, fortitude and endurance of our young sailors, soldiers, airmen and the men of the Merchant Marine who, 8,000 miles from home without a base, in tempestuous wintry seas stormed and liberated a rocky archipelago, held by a strongly dug-in and well-equipped invading force nearly twice as large. Faced by a flagrant breach of International Law and the invasion of a small, self-governing British community by a military dictatorship notorious for its inhuman treatment of dissidents, Britain's Prime Minister realised that it was no longer a question of whether we could afford to operate a surface fleet in such distant waters, but whether we could afford not to. By her courage and resolution she reminded a people, who for a generation had forgotten it, that the finest moments in their past had been those when they had staked their own safety to defend the liberties of the weak against the strong. The words, *Task Force South*, reminded England that she had a soul, and that her island situation and ocean-wide commerce made her dependent on naval ability to respond flexibly to any challenge at sea.

For during the Falklands campaign, regardless of the risks we were running, the Royal Navy put ashore on a hostile coast in the course of a winter's night a fighting force, with its ancillary arms and supplies, of something like 5,000 men. This wonderful feat of arms, never surpassed in our long sea annals, was comparable to the achievement of Wolfe and his naval colleague when he carried his army, undetected, to the Heights of Abraham and so decided the future of Canada.

9

History teaches that there are times when only brave deeds can restrain evil acts. This, an unpopular truth today, is one which, in every generation, men have to learn during their brief sojourn on this earth of contending passions and conflicting needs and desires. No country hates war and violence more than Britain; 'all force', wrote the great seventeenth-century Lord Halifax, 'is a kind of foul play.' And, having our frontiers in the oceans and long enjoyed control of their surface to ensure our trading livelihood and our peace and freedom, we have developed a form of government—the very reverse of military dictatorship—based on free and peaceful discussion, on what our medieval ancestors called counsel and consent, in which every man is free to oppose and criticise his fellows and rulers, and in which national decision is only reached after full debate and criticism. In the last resort it is based on the rule of law freely arrived at in Parliament and enforced in our open courts. 'All our struggles for liberty', said Disraeli, 'smack of law.' Our freedom—the very breath of England's spirit—is set in a framework of law. That is why we always resist lawless violence, abroad as at home. An agreed discipline, never for its own sake or unilaterally enforced from above—the wasting disease of all dictatorships—but solely to preserve freedom with, what the English and British value above all things, justice.

Of the three periods into which our history falls, the most recent began around two hundred years ago when we started to make ourselves an industrial nation, dependent on our genius for creating and using machinery and selling its products in exchange for raw materials and food increasingly imported from abroad.

The most formative part of our long history was that in which the spirit of England grew out of the Christian faith and the political institutions which still provide the framework of our national society were formed—the monarchy, the Church, the parish, the Common Law, the beginnings of Parliament. For all their remoteness from us, what we call the Middle Ages have the power to strike a chord in any mind not entirely obsessed by the material and ephemeral. The fashions and manners and most of the beliefs which men then followed have long been abandoned or forgotten. Yet some remain, a towering testimony to the strength and permanence of the greatest of all their beliefs, their intense and abiding sense of the grandeur and immutability of God. To this day the vast cathedrals they made with their puny tools and child's machinery tower above the cities of modern Britain.

Between these two periods was a third which lasted for three or four centuries. A rustic society called England and later Britain, operating in the framework of political institutions which we still enjoy, created one of the two or three greatest cultures the world has ever seen. The fruits of that culture comprised the poetry of Chaucer, the Border Ballads, of Shakespeare, Donne, Milton, Dryden, Pope and, straying into the beginnings of our own age, of Blake, Wordsworth, Keats and Coleridge; the architecture of the Perpendicular church builders, of the makers of the English village and the Cotswold and East Anglian towns and great country houses, of Inigo Jones, Wren and Kent; the music of Dunstable, Byrd, Lawes, Purcell and Arne, and the rustic treasure of folk song and dance; the theology of the Nonconformist divines and the philosophy of Bacon, Newton and Locke; the faith of Langland, Bunyan and Wesley; and, above all, the sturdy morality, good sense and robust courage and skill of the English country gentleman, yeoman, peasant and craftsman.

All this is the theme of a far larger and more ambitious work than my present *Spirit of England*. For more than thirty years I have been engaged on a book which I had hoped by now to have published—*The Story of Britain*, a comprehensive history of Great Britain, following my old friend and master, G. M. Trevelyan, who in 1926 published a political *History of Britain* in one volume, and, in 1941, its brilliant sequel *English History 1340–1900*. But, unlike him, I am covering both in a single volume, both political and social. To do so I have been able to draw on seven carefully researched and closely written detailed historical narratives of my own written over the past fifty years.

In this larger book, now all but complete, I have chronicled our past in three broad divisions of time—'The Making of England' from 8000 B.C. to 1497; 'The British Ocean Expansion' from 1497 to 1815; and the third, which I have called 'A Search for Justice', from 1815 to 1940 and after. In the first, 'The Making of England', I have written, too, of the early history of the indomitable little neighbour nations which once fought against her and later became joined with her under the name of Great Britain. Theirs was the challenge which helped to make England, just as England's was the challenge which helped to make them. And I have sought to show how her history and theirs—and that of the ocean nations which later sprang from them—grew originally out of the Christian heritage of Western Europe. For the secret of England's history is that she has never been self-contained. She has received ideas and men, or sent them out to others.

The writing of history has become so specialised and the volume of material available so vast that to tell the story of Britain adequately in a single volume—or as I have elsewhere done in seven— has become a task to daunt even the boldest historian. No life is long enough to compass all the reading required for its foundation or to distil and reduce to literary form such an immense, and often conflicting, volume of learning. Yet 'the best is the enemy of the good', and in an age in which society depends on the knowledge and opinion of the many, at least some historians must try to present their country's past in a form capable of awakening the understanding and imagination of those who have to shape its present.

My coming *History of Great Britain* makes no claim to originality; it merely tells a familiar story in a new way. It is not a work of original scholarship, but only a collation of the scholarship of others, to whom my debt is incalculable. In it I have sought to combine, with quick-moving narrative and compressed fact and date, as much of that detailed and graphic reconstruction of the past as can alone convey its living reality to the present. I have taken as little for granted as possible, but have told the story as it unfolded itself to the living men and women of the time. Throughout I have tried to portray the outward appearance of their lives; to show how they lived and what our country looked like; to recall the warmth and actuality of an existence once as real as ours. In doing so I have written for young and old, for those who know a little of the British past and for those who know scarcely anything at all. My aim has been to set down in a small compass the essential things a child or adult should know who wants to understand our history, in a book which can be read at school and by the fireside, on a journey or in bed, to leave the reader with a clear picture of how our institutions, beliefs and ideals came to be what they are.

The key to the writing and teaching of history is to make the past real. A historian's business is to recreate the past and then to interpret it. He cannot do the second until he has done the first.

INTRODUCTION

The past only seems real when it is seen as actually happening to living men and women with the same capacity for perception and feeling as ourselves. That is what I call living history, and it is living history I have tried to present, both in my longer story of Britain to come and in this brief foretaste of it, *Spirit of England*.

Arthur Bryant
September 1982

PART ONE

STRONGER
THAN
THE STORMS

The Undying Flame

MY CALLING is the humdrum one of writing history and of trying to write it in such a way as to make it not only true but readable. It may not be a very creative form of literature but at least, like breaking stones, it involves plenty of hard work. It demands the collection of a vast array of facts from a large variety of sources—it is immaterial whether these are from original manuscripts or books, since the latter are only manuscripts already printed. It also involves the exercise of judgement; one has to weigh one's sources. And it demands a certain professional integrity and the application of rules which experience has shown to be necessary in assessing historical material. Beyond that the thing is comparatively simple; it requires merely time and industry—a very large amount of both.

But that is only the beginning. What is far harder is to make the result of one's researches interesting to others; to put them in such a way that the reader finds it hard to lay the narrative or argument down. And this involves a further and more exacting labour: that of constantly writing and re-writing until a mass of ill-arranged, undigested material can be reduced to simple, logical prose; prose, that is, in which every sentence leads the reader naturally and irresistibly to the next, every paragraph to the next paragraph and every chapter to the next.

Those who essay this art know what is the historian's chief enemy. It is weariness; lack of vitality; the loss of the first fine careless rapture, vision, and resolve in a mass of paper under which one's spirits and body sink. And at such times I have found the immense value of great literature. Again and again there comes to the historian's rescue out of his documents—out of the dead hand of the past—the inspiration of genius: that of some long dead man or woman who knew how to convey truth and reality, not in some interminable rig-marole, but in a few phrases which shine across the centuries like a searchlight.

For the function of literature is to convey emotion, experience, or meaning in the fewest possible words. The necessity for doing so lies in a limitation of human nature—one with which we are all familiar. Seldom bored by their own experience or ideas, human beings possess an extremely low resistance to boredom by those of others: and, once such boredom sets in, their attention ceases altogether. The writer or speaker loses his audience. This applies particularly to the relationship between writer and reader. In conversation a communicator can at least fix his victim with a magnetic eye and hold his attention against his will; or the latter out of courtesy may listen long after his interest has flagged. But the writer has no such advantage. His reader is restricted neither by courtesy nor fear. He tends to ignore the writer's communication as soon as he finds it tedious. He puts the book down, or throws it away. However important the rest of the writer's communication, it is never communicated. Hence the necessity for the art we call literature—of delighting and holding the reader. The soul of wit is brevity—and so is the soul of literature. Most books published are two or three times too long.

Literary contributions to the historian's store may take many forms. It may be that of a first-hand account of some great public event which enables the scholar at his midnight oil perhaps centuries later to see it with the same clarity and freshness. Such was Samuel Pepys's description of the Fire of London or Creevey's of his meeting with Wellington in a Brussels square before Waterloo. Or it may be a lightning picture of some great historical figure—a portrait drawn in a phrase. It helps a historian to know that a contemporary of Elizabeth of Bohemia wrote of her as 'th' eclipse and glory of her kind.' So does Philip Warwick's description of his first sight of Cromwell speaking in the House with the spot of blood on his collar, or Charles Lamb's of Nelson walking down Pall Mall just before he embarked for Trafalgar. Sometimes, too, a man who is himself the theme of history and happens to be a born writer will reveal himself in a phrase, as when Montrose tells us:

> He either fears his fate too much
> Or his deserts are small,
> That dares not put it to the touch
> To gain or lose it all.

Another aid to the historian is the phrase in which a writer summarises a historical situation, as when the great Lord Halifax wrote, in a letter, of the politicians at the time of the Popish Plot

> They like a flood break down all.

Another, usually to be found in poetry, is the

expression of public mood: a very elusive thing to grasp in any other way. A supreme example are Walter Scott's lines in the Introduction to *Marmion* in which he draws the loneliness and isolation of Britain at the height of her struggle with Napoleon after the death in quick succession of Pitt, Fox, and Nelson.

> But oh! my country's wintry state
> What second spring shall renovate?
> What powerful call shall bid arise
> The buried warlike, and the wise? . . .
>
> Now is the stately column broke,
> The beacon-light is quench'd in smoke,
> The trumpet's silver sound is still,
> The warder silent on the hill!

But for such lines, though the same sense may be expressed in innumerable uninspired letters, the historian, impressed by the greatness of our victory at Trafalgar and with his foreknowledge of what was to happen, might fail to appreciate the depth of the nation's despondency at the death, so soon after one another, of Nelson and Pitt and, with it, the courage and resolution with which it was surmounted.

There is so much in the historian's province, as there is in life itself, that is intangible and which only great art can still communicate when it is 'vanished into air, into thin air'. How, for instance, could one wholly understand the medieval mind, with its sense of the mystery of life and death, without such a great poem as the 'Lyke-Wake Dirge'?

> If ever thou gavest meat or drink
> —Every night and all,
> The fire shall never make thee shrink;
>   And Christ receive thy soul . . .

This ae night, this ae night,
—Every night and all,
Fire and fleet and candle-light,
    And Christ receive thy soul.

Let me take a few examples from English literature which enlarge our comprehension of the course of our history. It is hard, of course, to find much inspiration of this kind in our very early history because the men and women who lived then did not speak our language or, at any rate, only a variant of it that we can only just understand. The first unmistakable note of genius conveying past English experience in our tongue is, I think, the Battle of Maldon, in which a thousand years ago an anonymous poet described how Britnoth, earl of Essex, and his thanes died fighting to the last man as the Danes closed round,

Thought shall be the harder,
        heart the keener,
Mood shall be the more,
        as our might lessens.

Through the cloud of pedantically spelt and outlandish names inflicted on generations of British students, he makes us see the manliness of the folk he was writing about; their steadfastness and loyalty, their readiness to die for cause and comrade, in the last ditch, even when there was no longer any hope of victory. He makes us realise, with pride and recognition, that *these* were our ancestors. Theirs was a rough, masculine creed without much subtlety or refinement. But it was the kind which bred in men a sense of duty and responsibility without which no nation can be great or endure. It makes the Anglo-Saxons real to us to see them in that doomed ring in the Essex marshes. So does the testimony of the

Norman chronicler describing the last hours at Hastings. 'In the English ranks the only movement was the dropping of the dead; the living stood motionless . . . They were ever ready with their steel, those sons of the old Saxon race, the most dauntless of men.'

For nearly three centuries after their defeat at Hastings the English are a silent people. They speak, but their speech is not written down, for all writing in England, or nearly all, is done in French or Latin. The Anglo-Saxon chronicler, writing in his cell—almost the last of his line before the French flood submerged the old national tongue—enables us to see the great Conqueror—'so stark a man'—who had laid England low. 'So stern was he and hot that no man durst do anything against his will.' And who that read it is likely to forget his description of the 'geld exceeding stiff' which he laid on as soon as he was crowned? Or the chronicler's—and taxpayer's—disgust at his later meticulous Domesday inquisition? 'So narrowly did he cause the survey to be made that there was not one single hide or rood of land, nor—it is shameful to tell, but he thought it no shame to do—was there an ox, cow or swine that was not set down in the writ.' One can feel the hatred for William in this brilliant picture of him by the representative of a conquered, scourged people, but one can feel the admiration that he attracted, too.

For the most part, from the reign of William the Conqueror until that of Edward III we have to rely for our history on great passages from French or Latin sources. Yet once or twice, behind the scenes of the life of the great and learned, we hear from below the salt the sturdy vernacular of country England. The earliest echoes that come to us down the corridors of time are

in verse: from Gloucestershire in the thirteenth
century—

> Where is Paris and Heleyne
> That were so bright and fair of blee?

or Robin Hood's joy in the flowering of the green
wood:

> In summer when the shawes be sheynë
> And leavës be large and long,
> It is full merry in fair forest
> To hear the fowlys' song.

Such verses tell us something about our ancestors that
we can obtain from no other source. They are as
important as the shape of their fields, the rules of their
communal cultivations, the customs of their local
courts and laws. And, as we listen, we see for a moment
their outward form: shepherds on the hills at lambing
and sheep-shearing, or driving their flocks at dusk into
great stone sheepcotes; foresters in green jerkins with
bows and arrows; spinsters turning their wheels at
open doors on summer evenings. By what they sang we
can tell what Englishmen loved.

And then in the last half of the fourteenth century
two great English writers appear and interpret their age
for us. In their personal experience and outlook, there
could scarcely have been two men more unlike than
Chaucer, the rich London vintner's son and court
official, and Langland, the poor West Country
chantry-clerk. Yet between them they present us with
an almost complete picture of the ordinary Englishman
in the reign of Richard II. Each has something, from the
historian's point of view, of supreme importance to
say. Langland, the puritan and reformer, from his
visionary viewpoint on the Malvern hills, gazing out

over the vast 'field full of folk'—and what antiquarian ever coined a more telling description of the medieval common field?—makes us see what Englishmen in their serious moments felt about their society, what they thought was wrong with it, and how they felt it ought to be reformed. He makes us realise, as no economist can, that the national *malaise* after the Black Death was spiritual. It was a sickness of soul of a people who felt that justice—their ideal—was somehow being outraged.

And if Langland makes us see why the English peasantry of the fourteenth century revolted—and there were plenty of good economic reasons—and why the orthodox and unideologically minded English were beginning to turn against the international Church—and there were plenty of theological reasons—Chaucer's poetry reveals something even more significant. It enables us to understand why, when it came to England, revolution proved so much more human, fair-tempered, and on the whole transient than elsewhere. For if Langland communicates to us the English soul in the fourteenth century, Chaucer enables us to see the unchanging Englishman himself, firmly set against the unfamiliar scenery of a vanished age. In a still anonymous time—that of the Cathedral, the Guild, and the Corporation—he showed us that the Englishman was already what he has so long been: an individual. Before the characters of the first commoners emerge from the flat, two-dimensional horizon of medieval history, this unassuming civil servant, with his observant eye and all-embracing charity, proclaimed their separate identity. The Wife of Bath is as great a historical phenomenon as Thomas à Becket or Robert Bruce, even though in one sense she never existed. Chaucer created a whole world of imaginary yet living characters. We see them riding through the Kentish countryside: the big, boastful, drunken miller with his bristly, red beard, and the tufted hairs on his nose; mine host of the Tabard chaffing and cajoling everyone into telling his story; the friar familiar with all the householders along the road and their wives and daughters, and his foe, the summoner, with his pimples, fiery, spotted face, and garlic-laden breath. Every pilgrim appears in turn as a complete and separate being. To each of them, sketched in a few brilliant lines, is given a story to tell so exquisitely in part that it unfolds the teller's very soul. It was fitting that before the great painters of Burgundy, Italy, and Flanders, an English poet should have been the first to do this thing. For of all the lands of Europe none had given more freedom to the individual than England.

It is when we come to the Tudors, and, above all, to the reign of Elizabeth, that we find ourselves in the full stream of English literature. It seemed almost impossible at that time for an Englishman to open his mouth or put pen to paper without saying something which brings his age back into the room. And the words of its greater spirits burn like flame. So Francis Drake, looking out from his portrait at Greenwich like a cheerful and prosperous grocer, writes to the Government that the wings of opportunity are fledged with the feathers of death. What dozen other words could so wonderfully epitomise the spirit of an age? And the great Queen herself, drawing her picture in a few paragraphs which are themselves an autobiography! 'I will never be by violence constrained to do anything. I thank God I am endued with such qualities that if I were turned out of my realm in my petticoat I were able to live in any place in Christendom!' . . . 'I know I have but the body of a weak and feeble woman; but I have the heart of a king, and of a King of England, too; and think scorn that Parma or Spain, or any Prince of Europe, should dare to invade the borders of my realm.' That was the way that Gloriana ruled England, and she herself has told us how.

It would not be hard to tell the story of England since the sixteenth century entirely from great passages by great English writers. Let me take, at random, a few extracts from our prose and poetry to show what I mean. Thus the great struggle of the seventeenth century can be resolved in a few lines of prose or verse—the cavalier, Sir Bevil Grenville's 'I cannot contain myself within my doors when the King of England's standard waves in the field upon so just an occasion—the cause being such as must make all those who die in it little inferior to martyrs.' And on the other side, Cromwell after Marston Moor: 'Truly England and the Church of God hath had a great favour from the Lord in this great Victory given unto us, such as the like never was since this War began . . . We never charged but we routed the enemy . . . God made them as stubble to our swords.' Old Sir Jacob Astley, almost the last to give up the game, sitting down on the drum in the market square at Stow-in-the-Wold to say to his captors: 'Well, gentlemen; you have done your business. You can go now play—if you fall not out among yourselves!' And three years later the King on his trial in Westminster Hall and the axe turned towards him: 'It is not my case alone; it is the freedom and liberty of the people of England. And do you pretend what you will—I must justly stand for their liberties. For if power without law may make law, may alter the fundamental laws of the Kingdom, I do not know what subject he is in England can be assured of his life or anything he can call his own.'

Let the poet, Marvell, in his great 'Horatian Ode' to Cromwell, take up the tale:

> 'Tis madness to resist or blame
> The force of angry Heaven's flame;
>   And if we would speak true,
>   Much to the man is due,
>
> Who, from his private gardens, where
> He liv'd reserved and austere
>   (As if his highest plot
>   To plant the bergamot),
>
> Could by industrious valour climb
> To ruin the great work of time,
>   And cast the Kingdoms old
>   Into another mould . . .
>
> That thence the Royal actor borne
> The tragic scaffold might adorn:
>   While round the armed bands
>   Did clap their bloody hands.
>
> He nothing common did or mean
> Upon that memorable scene,
>   But with his keener eye
>   The axe's edge did try;
>
> Nor call'd the Gods, with vulgar spite,
> To vindicate his helpless right;
>   But bow'd his comely head
>   Down, as upon a bed . . .

What may not then our Isle presume
While victory his crest does plume?
    What may not others fear,
    If thus he crown each year? . . .

But thou, the War's and Fortune's son,
March indefatigably on;
    And for the last effect,
    Still keep the sword erect;

Besides the force it has to fright
The spirits of the shady night,
    The same arts that did gain
    A power, must it maintain.

Must it maintain? Yes, nine years later, that power
having failed to maintain itself in face of ever-growing
passive resistance, young Mr Pepys going home on the
day General Monk marched into the City and declared
for a free Parliament, counted thirty bonfires in a
single street, 'Indeed, it was past imagination, both the
greatness and the suddenness of it!'

And the Restoration. Did the chapter end there?
And if not can the genius of our literature continue it?

Let us drink and be merry, dance, joke, and rejoice,
With claret and sherry, theorbo and voice!
The changeable world, to our joy is unjust,
    All treasure's uncertain
    Then down with your dust!
In frolics dispose your pounds, shillings and pence,
For we shall be nothing a hundred years hence.

We'll sport and be free with Moll, Betty, and Dolly,
Have oysters and lobsters to cure melancholy:
Fish-dinners will make a man spring like a flea,
    Dame Venus, love's lady,
    Was born of the sea;

With her and with Bacchus we'll tickle the sense,
For we shall be past it a hundred years hence.

The sons of Belial, in short, flown with insolence and
wine! No! The chapter continues—in an old blind poet,
once Latin secretary to the Lord Protector,

> All is best, though we oft doubt
> What th' unsearchable dispose
> Of highest wisdom brings about,
> And ever best found in the close.
> Oft he seems to hide his face,
> But unexpectedly returns
> And to his faithful Champion hath in place
> Bore witness gloriously; whence Gaza mourns
> And all that band them to resist
> His uncontroulable intent.
> His servants he with new acquist
> Of true experience from this great event
> With peace and consolation hath dismist,
> And calm of mind all passion spent.

Yes; and a tinker in Bedford jail who once served in the
Roundhead garrison of Newport Pagnell and, in
disgrace with the new order, is at work on a book
whose first edition, three centuries later, was to fetch
more in an auction room that any other English book
ever sold.

> After this, it was noised abroad, that Mr. *Valiant-for-
> Truth* was taken with a summons by the same post as
> the other; and had this for a token that the summons
> was true, *That his pitcher was broken at the fountain.*
> When he understood it, he called for his friends, and
> told them of it. Then, said he, I am going to my Father's
> and tho' with great difficulty I am got hither, yet now I
> do not repent me of all the trouble I have been at to
> arrive where I am. *My Sword* I give to him that shall
> succeed me in my Pilgrimage, and my *Courage* and

Skill to him that can get it. My *marks* and *scars* I carry with me, to be a witness for me, that I have fought His battles, who now will be my Rewarder. When the day that he must go hence was come, many accompany'd him to the River-side, into which as he went, he said, *Death, where is thy Sting?* And as he went down deeper, he said, *Grave, where is thy Victory?* So he passed over, and all the Trumpets sounded for him on the other side.

No: not the *end* of the chapter! Chapters never end in history, so long as nobility in the defeated can find such words to awake victory in the unborn.

Let us leave these high levels, as the England of the Restoration left them—to lay out St. James's Park, build St. Paul's, write the *Principia* and compose *Dido and Aeneas.* Let us go down the river with John Dryden, the poet, during the crisis of the second Dutch War—a war fought for *commerce.*

It was that memorable day, in the first summer of the late War, when our Navy engaged the Dutch; a day wherein the two most mighty and best-appointed Fleets which any age had ever seen, disputed the command of the greater half of the Globe, the commerce of nations, and the riches of the Universe. While these vast floating bodies, on either side, moved against each other in parallel lines, and our Countrymen . . . went breaking, little by little, into the line of the Enemies; the noise of the cannon from both Navies reached our ears about the City, so that all men being alarmed with it, and in a dreadful suspense of the event which we knew was then deciding, every one went following the sound as his fancy led him; and leaving the Town almost empty, some took towards the Park, some cross the River, others down it; all seeking the noise in the depth of silence . . .

For in the second half of the seventeenth century the Navy had become very important to Englishmen. Under Elizabeth it had saved them from the Armada; since then it had enabled them to found new Englands beyond the oceans and to open up trade in every corner of the world. And it had enabled them, secure behind the moat it guarded, to wrestle with one another for their parliamentary liberties at a time when all Europe was becoming the prey of despotic monarchy.

> It may be said now to England, Martha, Martha, thou art busy about many things, but one thing is necessary. To the question, what shall we do to be saved in this World? there is no other answer but this, Look to your Moat.
>
> The first Article of an Englishman's Political Creed must be, That he believeth in the Sea . . .
>
> We are in an Island, confined to it by God Almighty, not as a Penalty but a Grace, and one of the greatest that can be given to Mankind. Happy confinement, that hath made us Free, Rich and Quiet; a fair Portion in this World, and very well worth the preserving.

Lord Halifax's lesson was not forgotten by our ancestors. It was the cause of their wealth and freedom. If we want to understand the realisation of it we cannot do better than turn to a passage in the last work of one of our first great novelists, Henry Fielding, describing his voyage down the Thames on his way to Lisbon. The Navy, patriotism, and liberty were very closely connected in the minds of eighteenth-century Englishmen. And what the English meant by liberty we can find in the work of another great writer of the period. 'From this neglect of subordination', Dr Johnson wrote of the turbulence of the London mob, 'I do not deny that some inconveniences may from time to time proceed ... But good and evil will grow up in the world together; and they who complain in peace of the insolence of the populace, must remember that their insolence in peace is bravery in war.'

It was through forgetfulness of the fact that Englishmen insist, wherever they live, on enjoying liberty that in the latter eighteenth century England lost the first British Empire. And at the moment she lost it a great Irish writer, Edmund Burke, stated from the Opposition benches the principle which enabled her to create and retain the second British Empire: today the Commonwealth.

My hold of the Colonies is in the close affection which grows from common names, from kindred blood, from similar privileges, and equal protection. These are ties which, though light as air, are as strong as links of iron. Let the colonists always keep the idea of their civil rights associated with your government—they will cling and grapple to you; and no force under heaven will be of power to tear them from their allegiance ... As long as you have the wisdom to keep the sovereign authority of this country as the sanctuary of liberty, the sacred temple consecrated to our common faith, wherever the chosen race and sons of England worship freedom, they will turn their faces towards you. The more they multiply, the more friends you will have; the more ardently they love liberty, the more perfect will be their obedience. Slavery they can have anywhere. It is a weed that grows in every soil. They may have it from Spain, they may have it from Prussia. But until you become lost to all feeling of your true interest and your natural dignity, freedom they can have from none but you.

For twenty-two years England, or Britain as she had become, fought for that liberty against Revolutionary

France and Napoleon. That epic story could be told in the words almost of one poet alone—Wordsworth: hailing the first deluding hopes of the Revolution, 'walking the old green hills' dogged by Pitt's spies; watching at Calais the stream of well-meaning English appeasers flocking to Paris to pay their court to Napoleon; returning to England in the Dover packet knowing in his bones that war was certain:

> Here, on our native soil, we breathe once more.
> The cock that crows, the smoke that curls, that sound
> Of bells—those boys who in yon meadow-ground
> In white-sleeved shirts are playing; and the roar
> Of the waves breaking on the chalky shore—
> All, all are English. Oft have I looked round
> With joy in Kent's green vales; but never found
> Myself so satisfied in heart before.
> Europe is yet in bonds, but let that pass,
> Thought for another moment. Thou art free,
> My Country!

A few weeks before war broke out there appeared in the *Morning Post* another poem under the same name:

> It is not to be thought of that the flood
> Of British freedom, which, to the open sea
> Of the world's praise, from dark antiquity
> Hath flowed, 'with pomp of waters, unwithstood,'—
> Roused though it be full often to a mood
> Which spurns the check of salutary bands,
> That this most famous stream in bogs and sands
> Should perish; and to evil and to good
> Be lost for ever. In our halls is hung
> Armoury of the invincible knights of old.
> We must be free or die who speak the tongue
> That Shakespeare spake, the faith and morals hold
> That Milton held.

It would be easy to make a selection of great passages from English literature to describe the century which followed: the wealth, the power, the expanding trade, the dark slum reverse of the commercial empire which led the world that, thanks to Britain, Napoleon had failed to conquer. There are many: I will confine myself to one. It is from the work of a Pole of genius who served in the British Merchant Marine at the end of Victoria's reign and who wrote English prose as only the very greatest of English writers have done. In this passage Joseph Conrad describes a ship coming up the Channel in the last days of sail.

The *Narcissus* entered the chops of the Channel . . . The clouds raced with her mastheads . . . the coast to welcome her stepped out of space into the sunshine . . . At night the headlands retreated, the bays advanced into one unbroken line of gloom. The lights of the earth mingled with the lights of heaven; and above the tossing lanterns of a trawling fleet a great lighthouse shone steadily, such as an enormous riding light burning above a vessel of fabulous dimensions. Below its steady glow, the coast, stretching away straight and black, resembled the high side of an indestructible craft riding motionless upon the immortal and unresting sea. The dark land lay alone in the midst of waters, like a mighty ship bestarred with vigilant lights—a ship carrying the burden of millions of lives—a ship freighted with dross and with jewels, with gold and with steel. She towered up immense and strong, guarding priceless traditions and untold suffering, sheltering glorious memories and base forgetfulness, ignoble virtues and splendid transgressions. A great ship! For ages had the ocean battered in vain her enduring sides; she was there when the world was vaster and darker, when the sea was great and mysterious, and ready to surrender the prize of fame to

audacious men. A ship mother of fleets and nations!
The great flagship of the race; stronger than the storms;
and anchored in the open sea.

She was still there in 1914—and in 1940—and it was
well for the world's liberty that she was.

The age between those two wars, like our own, saw
England in revolution. Turn back for a moment to
H. G. Wells's prophetic vision in his description of a
destroyer going down the Thames at the end of his
novel *Tono-Bungay*. He describes Craven Reach with
its trees and memories of the old England departing,
then the squalid reaches of mean homes and dingy
industrialism and the polite houses of the professional
classes in Chelsea, then the great mile at Westminster
'with its new hotels over-shadowing its Georgian and
Victorian architecture, and mud and great warehouses
and factories, chimneys, shot towers, adver-
tisements . . .' And then, 'soaring up, hanging in the
sky over a rude tumult of warehouses, over a jostling
competition of traders, irrelevantly beautiful and
altogether remote, Saint Paul's! . . .'

> And then the traditional and ostensible England falls
> from you altogether. The third movement begins, the
> last great movement in the London symphony, in
> which the trim scheme of the old order is altogether
> dwarfed and swallowed up . . . The great warehouses
> tower up about you waving stupendous cranes, the
> gulls circle and scream in your ears, large ships lie
> among their lighters, and one is in the port of the
> world . . .
> And you come at last with the sun behind you into
> the eastern sea . . . The hills of Kent . . . fall away on
> the right hand and Essex on the left. They fall away and

vanish into blue haze . . . And now behind us is blue mystery and the phantom flash of unseen lights, and presently even these are gone, and I and my destroyer tear out to the unknown across a great gray space. We tear into the great spaces of the future and the turbines fall to talking in unfamiliar tongues. Out to the open we go, to windy freedom and trackless ways. Light after light goes down. England and the Kingdom, Britain and the Empire, the old prides and the old devotions, glide abeam, astern, sink down upon the horizon, pass—pass. The river passes—London passes, England passes . . .

Yes: and a poet, Hilaire Belloc, speaks—

> Sally is gone that was so kindly,
>   Sally is gone from Ha'nacker Hill.
> And the Briar grows ever since then so blindly
>   And ever since then the clapper is still,
> And the sweeps have fallen from Ha'nacker Mill.
>
> Ha'nacker Hill is in Desolation:
>   Ruin a-top and a field unploughed.
> And Spirits that call on a falling nation:
>   Spirits that loved her calling aloud:
> Spirits abroad in a windy cloud.
>
> Spirits that call and no one answers;
>   Ha'nacker's down and England's done.
> Wind and Thistle for pipe and dancers
>   And never a ploughman under the Sun;
> Never a ploughman. Never a one.

But we have not come to the end of the story—the prophecies have been fulfilled—the seers have been proved right—and the hour of doom has struck. And the voice of England speaks out of darkness, and it is still the maker of great literature who speaks for her:

'We shall go on to the end ... We shall defend our Island, whatever the cost may be. We shall fight on the beaches, we shall fight on the landing grounds, we shall fight in the fields and in the streets; we shall fight in the hills; we shall never surrender ... You ask what is our aim? I can answer in one word; Victory—Victory at all costs. Victory in spite of all terrors; Victory, however hard and long the road may be; for without victory there is no survival.'

And because of those words, there was victory, and there was survival.

2

A Nursery for Freedom

Trackway and camp and city lost,
Salt marsh where now is corn,
Old wars, old peace, old arts that cease,
And so was England born.

Kipling

ENGLISH, the tongue of Shakespeare and Milton, and today the international language of half the world, including the United States of America and the Commonwealth which has grown out of the former British Empire, was originally a tribal vernacular and peasant patois of part of a small offshore island created by an Atlantic flood which, eight thousand years ago, cut it off from the European mainland. Colonised by a succession of seafaring invaders from that mainland, the island's most accessible and fertile area became the kingdom of England just over a thousand years ago, while its Caledonian moorlands about the same time became the kingdom of Scotland. Because of the security given by the moat of stormy tidal water surrounding the island, its peoples, and those of the small Celtic principalities of its western and northern mountains, were able, together, to develop a polity in which the sanctity of the individual counted for more than central authority, and in which power, instead of being concentrated in a few hands, was distributed in many.

Yet immense though its consequences, Britain's immunity from invasion is comparatively recent. Though an island geographically for eight thousand years, it has been one strategically for only a few hundred. It was made the first by Providence; it became the second through its people's efforts. At first no island was so easy to invade; none was more tempting to invaders. Iberian and Neolithic men, Bronze Age pastoral warriors, Celts, Romans, Jutes, Angles and Saxons, Danes, Norwegians, and Normans, all in turn descended on it, bringing death, enslavement, and destruction. A short voyage up its rivers could carry their war-boats to its heart. Its eight thousand miles of deeply indented coastline was indefensible by a small population fighting on land. It could only be defended by sea. And since its southern and eastern lowlands closest to the European continent were easiest to conquer and cultivate, each invader tended to settle there, driving earlier comers into the mountains, bogs, and mists of the west, where—since these offered very little to tempt conquerors—they survived.

The colonisers of Britain were confronted by a wet, windswept northern island. Even when they had won the land from their predecessors, they had to win a tougher and longer battle against Nature. They had to fell dense forests, covering at first the entire lowlands, clear and drain swampy river valleys, and break up the thick cold clays with implements, the making of which called for all their skill and ingenuity. Yet though it

offered them much to master, the climate was never too
harsh to endure. It steeled, but did not ossify, stamina
and character. Gusty and invigorating, it was tempered
by a warm ocean stream from the south-west which
usually spared the island continental winters. The soil,
infinitely varied, was nearly all fertile. It bred vigorous, hardy, adaptable plants, beasts, and men.

The survival of racial minorities, defying yet
ultimately intermarrying with the predominant majority, together with the island climate and situation,
shaped English history. Long skull and broad mingled,
short build and tall, dark pigmentation and blonde; so
did the instincts and memories of a score of races. Such
intermixture in so small an island helped to make its
people many-sided and versatile. Left to themselves the
Anglo-Saxons of a thousand years ago—florid, large-
limbed, blue-eyed, phlegmatic—might have settled
down into a sluggish complacency. But they were
harried by the Danes and Norsemen, and later
conquered by the Normans. In face of these powerful
minorities they had to struggle for centuries to retain
their customs, institutions, and language. And beyond
their well-ploughed shires, and in the hills, marshes,
and woodlands in their midst, lurked the pre-Saxon
inhabitants of the island—fierce red-haired Celts and
little dark Neolithic and Bronze Age peoples with
rugged irregular features, loose mouths, and deep-set
eyes. They, too, constituted a perpetual challenge to
the dominant majority, their Highland and Cymric
raids and the alluring, alien ways of their young men
and maidens bringing deeper and more mysterious
strains into the blood of the honest, ox-like Saxons.
The island was full of unexpected and mysterious
influences—Wendish customs among the sandy Surrey

gravels beside the Thames at Wandsworth, Scandina-
vian usages in the Chilterns, ancient pre-Roman and
even pre-Celtic settlements in hollows on the lonely
Wiltshire and Dorset downs. And along the marches of
the Celtic west and north ran the incessant, challenging
warfare of the races:

> When Severn down to Buildwas ran
> Coloured with the death of man,
> Couched upon her brother's grave
> The Saxon got me on the slave . . .
>
> In my heart it has not died,
> The war that sleeps on Severn side;
> They cease not fighting, east and west,
> On the marches of my breast

It is perhaps this which has accounted for the
intermixture in the British blood of the matter-of-fact
with the poetic; of love of home with the itch to
adventure; of business aptitude with fantasy, specula-
tion, and idealism. English literature is full of examples
of this conflict in the national make-up; of books
like *Alice in Wonderland* written by a professor of
mathematics, or *A Shropshire Lad* by a clerk in the
Patent Office who became a master of Latin philo-
logy. 'Lord', prayed the commander of the royalist
foot at Edgehill, 'Thou knowest how busy I shall be
this day; if I forget Thee, do not Thou forget me. March
on, boys!' So too Cromwell, on the other side, bade his
men trust in God and keep their powder dry. The
British—and more particularly the English in whom
the mingling of the races has been most marked—have
often been charged with hypocrisy, with serving both
God and Mammon, with trying to eat their cake and

have it. Since they have so many sides to their nature, there has been truth in the charge. Yet, in a world in which spirit and matter are inextricable, it has not served them badly. Their greatest poet wrote that men were such stuff as dreams are made on, yet contrived by sound business methods to make a competence in real property.

This clash of racial characteristics and cultures may have accounted, too, for the extraordinary range of British genius; in politics, agriculture, and commerce, in literature and the arts, in craftsmanship, war, adventure, and colonisation. So much diversity among neighbours was a constant stimulus and education. 'No nation', wrote Emerson, 'was ever so rich in able men.' Shakespeare and Milton, Elizabeth I and Cromwell, Chatham and Churchill, Drake, Nelson, and Wellington, Wren, Purcell, Dr Johnson, Newton and Darwin; the inventor of the steam-engine, and the discoverers of the anaesthetic, electricity, and the atom, have been a remarkable harvest for one small island. And Washington, Jefferson, Lee, and Lincoln were of the same argumentative, versatile stock.

Yet England was fortunate that the invasions which gave her so mixed an ancestry were separated by long periods. This enabled each new influence to be digested and saved the island from anarchy. The sea-barrier, even before the islanders learnt to hold it, proved a better protection than a land frontier. And after the Norman Conquest the growing use by her kings of the sea for defence gave her almost complete freedom from armed invasion. The only invaders who settled in Britain thereafter were refugees flying to her shores from persecution: Flemings in the fourteenth and sixteenth centuries, Huguenots in the seventeenth century, Jews in the eighteenth and nineteenth centuries, West Indians and Pakistanis in our own day. The racial challenge became a purely internal one: of Norman, Saxon, and Celt, Englishman, Scotsman, Welshman, and Irishman, contending and competing with one another.

This, and the strong rule of her early kings—Norman, Plantagenet, and Tudor—gave the country, for all its diversity, an inherent unity. Beneath immense differences of speech, outlook, and custom there grew up, under protection of the Common Law within and the patrolled seas without, first an English, and, later, a British, identity. This cohesion existed side by side with the most strongly held and freely expressed differences of opinion. But it never failed to unite the islanders when any major threat arose from outside.

Even more striking than England's unity has been the freedom of individual choice on which it has been based. Not being threatened across a land frontier, her people—unlike those of the adjacent continent—had no need to entrust their rulers with standing military force or despotic rights over private liberties. Authority normally was exercised only after those subject to it had an opportunity to make their views known. From the Saxon *Witanagemot* to the nineteenth-century Parliament, from the village hustings and manor court to the trade union lodge and parish council, there was nearly always some working machinery by which those in authority could test the opinion of those over whom authority had to be exercised. Government has been conducted subject to the right of the governed to criticise and, within lawful limits, to oppose. 'His Majesty's Opposition' is the most characteristic, and certainly the most original of English contributions to politics; today the Leader of the Opposition is even paid by the State. However inefficient in the short run, such a system proved efficient in the long, because, by delegating responsibility, it trained men for it.

For, like the Americans after them, the English regarded the person—even if at first only the privileged person—as more important than any abstract ideal. The State, they felt, existed more for the individual than the individual for the State. Their history was a struggle for the freedom of individuals. It was fought for at every stage of their developing consciousness, from the barons' stand for Magna Carta to the Tolpuddle martyrs paying with transportation for the rural worker's right to combine against his employer.

England's rulers have often contended against this national distaste for authority. King John tried to repress his barons, Mary Tudor the early Protestants, King Charles his unruly Parliaments. The eighteenth-century landowners sought to extinguish the independent cultivators of the common-field village and were themselves later overtaken by the rich yeomen who became industrial capitalists. And the nineteenth-century manufacturers tried in vain to repress the trade unions of their rough, liberty-loving factory-hands.

Loving private liberty, yet finding that it could not exist without public order, the English devoted themselves to making the two compatible. Freedom within a framework of discipline became their ideal. They achieved it through the sovereignty of law. 'All our struggles for liberty,' wrote Disraeli, 'smack of law.' And by law the English meant an enforceable compact between themselves and their rulers, deriving not from unilaterally imposed force but from assent freely given. Both they and their American descendants constituted such Law, rather than the Executive, their ultimate sovereign.

This respect for law gradually made the English people, who might otherwise have been one of the most difficult to govern, one of the easiest: easy, that is, so long as they were governed lawfully. It became habitual to them to obey the law and see it enforced. Their inter-racial experience in a small island left them with a profound distrust of violence. 'Force is not a remedy', declared John Bright: 'all force', wrote the great seventeenth-century Lord Halifax, 'is a kind of foul play.' From this sprang the curious tolerance of a fighting people with strong convictions for minority opinions, non-conformity, and eccentricity. No other community has ever so richly rewarded its critics or been so indulgent to those it terms conscientious objectors.

Compromise, give-and-take, live-and-let-live thus became a national habit. The freedom of the Press was an English invention; so was the secret ballot which enabled a man to record an unpopular vote without danger to himself. The English, as self-opinionated as any people, mastered the lesson that they could only possess liberty for themselves by allowing it to others, enjoy the propagation of their own views by listening patiently to those of their neighbours'. 'Opinion in good men', wrote one of their poets, 'is but knowledge in the making.' 'I beseech you, in the bowels of Christ,' Cromwell implored the Scottish Calvinist dogmatists, 'think it possible you may be mistaken!'

This hard-learnt toleration, and all the tolerated eccentricity arising from it, have rested in the last resort on the Christian belief in the sanctity of the individual. It stemmed from the creed of personal responsibility to which, first the Celts of Wales, Ireland, and Scotland, and then the Anglo-Saxons of England, were won by the great missionaries of the fifth, sixth, and seventh centuries. At its core lay the thesis that every man, being free to choose between good and evil, was a soul of equal value in the eyes of God. It was this which gave rise to an Englishman's saying in the English revolution of the seventeenth century that the 'poorest he in England hath a life to live as the greatest he.'

From Sir Philip Sidney passing the cup to the dying soldier to Captain Oates walking into the blizzard to save his friends, from Richard Coeur-de-Lion forgiving the archer who shot him to the men of the Forty-third standing motionless on the deck of the sinking *Birkenhead* while the women and children were lowered in the boats, the common denominator of the nation's idealism has remained constant. It was expressed in the fourteenth-century *Piers Plowman*, in the seventeenth-century *Pilgrim's Progress* and in the nineteenth-century *Christmas Carol*. Langland, Bunyan, and Dickens all spoke with the same voice. Whenever England has been false to that voice she has been false to herself. The English, Disraeli said, have not committed fewer blunders than others, but, being free to criticise their rulers according to individual conscience, have shown themselves as a people more sensible of their errors. In the end it has usually been the English themselves who have made amends for their injuries to others and reformed the abuses they had perpetrated. 'I choose the people under whom we suffered forty years ago,' declared General Smuts in 1940, 'but who, when we were at their mercy, treated us as a Christian people!'

The virtues of England sprang from nature, but also

from conscious will. The English were what they were because deep down they wished to be. Their tradition derived from their ancient Catholic past. Its purpose at its highest was to make Christian men; gentle, generous, humble, valiant, and chivalrous. Its enduring ideals were justice, mercy, and charity. Shakespeare was not writing fantasy when he put into the mouth of John of Gaunt his vision of a

> Land of such dear souls, this dear, dear land:
> Dear for her reputation through the world,

he was merely defining the idealised character of his country.

Her institutions were moulded to make it easier for her people to attain that character. Within their framework they could live Christian lives without denying human needs and without constant conflict between their conscience and circumstance. A squire or merchant who treated his neighbours with a sense of responsibility could still prosper. As a result of long and unbroken Christian usage, it became natural to the English to live and work in a society in which moral responsibility existed. And when England broke with the Catholic past—partly out of a critical sense of its human imperfections—she still cherished the old ideal of a realm dedicated to the task of breeding just and gentle men. All that was best in Puritanism was an attempt to restate it. Without justice and charity there could be no England. That has remained, and remains, the historic and unchanging English vision.

3

Black Death Strikes

Death came driving after and all to dust pashed
Kings and knights, caesars and popes . . .
Many a lovely lady and leman of knights
Swooned and swelted for sorrow of Death's dints.

William Langland

THE SUMMER OF 1348 was exceptionally wet. The Leicester chronicler, Henry Knighton, attributed the incessant downpour to the wanton behaviour of ladies at tournaments. Dressed in men's attire 'in party-coloured tunics, one colour or pattern on the right side and another on the left, with short hoods that had pendants like ropes wound round their necks, and belts thickly studded with gold or silver,' he complained, 'a band of women would come to share the sport, sometimes to the number of forty or fifty ladies, of the fairest and comeliest (though I say not of the best) among the whole kingdom. There they spent and lavished their possessions and wearied their bodies with fooleries and wanton buffoonery . . . But God in this matter, as in all others, brought marvellous remedy, for He harassed the places and times appointed for such vanities by opening the floodgates of heaven with rain and thunder and lurid lightning and by unwanted blasts of tempestuous winds.'

Yet, as the monastic historian was quick to point out, the rain which wrecked the tournaments in honour of King Edward III's foundation of the Order of the Garter was the least of the evils awaiting England that summer. God had prepared a far more awful punishment for her. Eighteen months earlier, while the English, after their miraculous victory at Crécy and their spectacular conquests in France, were besieging Calais, another army two thousand miles away had been blockading a small Genoese grain port in the Crimea where a band of silk-traders, operating at the end of the seven-thousand mile caravan route to China, had taken refuge from the Tartar horsemen of the Steppes. Suddenly the besiegers had been struck down by a pestilence which, spreading everywhere throughout Tartary and known as 'the death', had begun, it was believed, in the putrefaction of unburied multitudes in earthquakes in China. Before they raised the siege the Tartars are said to have catapulted some infected corpses into the town.

What is certain is that the disease was carried into Europe at the end of 1347 or beginning of 1348 by Genoese ships trading with the Black Sea. No one knew its cause or even its nature, but it is now believed to have been the bubonic plague—a flea-borne epidemic of the black rat* which had invaded Europe from Asia at the time of the crusades and with which the wooden trading ships of the day were heavily infested.

---

* The communication of plague by the bite of the rat-flea was only fully realised at the beginning of the present century, during the succession of epidemics between 1897 and 1907 which carried off some four million people in British India.

By the time vessels that had called in the Crimea reached the Bosphorus and Mediterranean the plague was raging among their crews, and every port at which they touched became infected. It struck so suddenly that at first no one had time to escape; at Constantinople the Byzantine Emperor's heir was among its victims. The symptoms were a gangrenous inflammation of the lungs, vomiting and spitting blood, vilely infected breath and the appearance, on the second day, of hard black buboes in the arm-pits and groin which were almost always the heralds of death. Few who caught the disease in its first onslaught outlived the third day.

By the end of January 1348 the plague was raging in all the great ports of southern Europe, including Venice, Genoa, Marseilles and Barcelona. In the Mediterranean ships were found drifting with every member of the crew dead. One after another, despite frantic attempts to isolate themselves, the Italian cities went down before the pestilence. Terrifying stories circulated of its supernatural origin; of how 'in the east, hard by Greater India, fire and stinking smoke had burned up all the cities' and how 'between Cathay and Persia there had rained a vast rain of fire, falling in flakes like snow and burning up mountains and plains with men and women', and accompanied by a sinister black cloud that 'whosoever beheld died within the space of half a day.' Thence, borne by 'a foul blast of wind from the south', the infection had invaded Europe.

In the spring, having made Venice and Genoa cities of the dead, the plague reached Florence. In the introduction to his *Decameron* Boccaccio left a first-hand picture of its horrors: the helplessness of the doctors, the stench of the sick, the cautious shutting themselves up in their houses until the infection crept in and the reckless drinking in taverns day and night, the multitude of corpses lying uncovered before every church and the pits into which the dead were packed in layers. The poor perished in the streets or among the crops, the swine rooting in the deserted streets dropped dead as they nosed the bundles of rags stripped from the plague-stricken, and swarms of oxen, sheep and goats—'and even dogs, those most faithful friends to men'—wandered untended through the fields. The dying were abandoned, the dead were dragged out of the houses and stacked by the road-side, the houses of those who had fled were left open to all, 'the reverend authority of the laws, divine and human, being almost wholly ruined and dissolved.' It was the same virtually everywhere: in Siena, in Piacenza, in Parma, and in Rimini, where the chronicler, Agniolo di Tura, carried with his own hands his five little sons to the grave.

While the plague was devastating Italy, it spread in widening circles from the Mediterranean eastwards into Istria and Hungary and over the Alps into Bavaria, westwards across Spain where it struck down the Queen of Aragon and, later, the King of Castile, and northwards from Marseilles up the Rhône. It broke out in the convent of the Carmelite friars at Avignon before anyone even realised what it was, slaying Laura, the adored of the poet Petrarch, and the abbot of the great Canterbury monastery of St. Augustine's who was visiting the *curia* at the time. 'When anyone who is infected by it dies,' wrote a Flemish canon from the city, 'all who see him in his sickness or visit him or even carry him to the grave, quickly follow him there. The sick are served by their kinsfolk as dogs would be; food is put near the bed for them to eat and drink after which all fly . . . Nor do priests hear confessions or give the sacraments.' 'Charity was dead', reported the Pope's physician, who himself caught the disease and was one of the few to recover. 'Even the doctors did not dare to visit the sick. As for me, to avoid infamy, I did not dare to absent myself but still I was in continual fear.' The Pope, ordering corpses to be dissected to find the cause of the disease, fled to his country seat near Valence, where he shut himself up in a single room, keeping fires constantly burning to stifle the infection and giving access to no one.

All that summer of 1348 the Black Death was drawing nearer to England. In the spring it reached Gascony where it struck down King Edward's youngest daughter, the Princess Jean, who was on her way to Spain to marry the heir of Castile. Soon afterwards it broke out in Paris where vast multitudes died, including the Queens of France and Navarre. By July, creeping north through Poitou and Brittany and round the coasts, it was in Normandy, where 'it came to such a pass that no-one could be found even to carry the corpses to the tomb. People said that the end of the world had come.' All the while clouds and continuous rain poured down on England and, towards the end of the month as men watched the ports, Archbishop Zouche of York wrote to his deputy ordering processions and litanies to be held in all parish churches twice a week 'for the stay of pestilence and infection.' Only by prayer, he declared, could the scourge be turned away.

The Archbishop—the victor of Neville's Cross— spoke of man's life being a warfare, where 'those fighting amidst the miseries of this world are troubled by the uncertainty of a future now propitious, now averse, the Lord Almighty permitting those whom he loves to be chastised so that strength by the infusion of spiritual grace may be made perfect in infirmity.' But though the Bishop of Bath and Wells, equally apprehensive, ordered processions and stations in all his churches to 'protect the people from the pestilence which had come from the East into the neighbouring kingdom', life in England that summer seems to have gone on very much as usual. In days when news travelled only by word of mouth and was carried from village to village along the grass roadways by friars and pedlars, the people of an isolated northern island can have heard little of the fate which had befallen their fellow Christians beyond the Channel. Absorbed in their local affairs, they were more concerned about the weather, the ruin of their crops and the murrain that had broken out among the sheep and cattle. Even the King, who must have been fully aware of the danger, seemed obsessed with his magnificent building projects for housing the college of his new Order of the Garter. On 6 August, he issued orders for the conversion of St. Edward the Confessor's chapel, Windsor, into one 'of befitting splendour' and for the provision of accommodation for the additional canons and twenty-four 'helpless and indigent knights' whom he and his companions were to present on the next St. George's Day 'in honour of Almighty God and of his mother Mary the glorious Virgin and of St. George the Martyr.'

It may have been on that very day that, despite every precaution by the port authorities, the plague crossed the Channel. Some time early in August it broke out in the little Dorset coast town of Melcombe Regis, now Weymouth, 'depriving it almost of inhabitants'. Within a few weeks it reached Bristol, probably by sea, turning it into a cemetery. It treated England as it had treated western Europe, and the English reacted in the same way. At Bristol 'the living were scarce able to bury the dead', and 'the men of Gloucester would not suffer the Bristol men to have access to them.' But no constable's guard could stop the swift-running rats from infecting one another, or their parasites from deserting their putrescent bodies for living men and women. Nor had anyone any idea what caused the mortality: the pallor, the sudden shivering and retching, the dreaded scarlet botches and black boils—'God's tokens'—the delirium and unbearable agony which came without warning and carried off its victims in a few hours.

During that autumn the plague struck down southern shire after shire. Dorset and its adjoining counties suffered terribly; Poole was so depopulated that it did not recover for more than a century—a hundred years ago a projecting strip of land known as the Baiter was still pointed out as the burial-place of its victims. In some villages, like Bishopstone in Wiltshire, scarcely a soul survived, and when life was renewed after the plague the site was left deserted. The crops rotted in the fields, the church bells were silent, and everywhere corpses were flung, blackened and stinking, into hastily dug pits. At his lonely episcopal manor of Wiveliscombe, where he and his *familia* remained during the visitation, the Bishop of Bath and Wells instituted an endless succession of incumbents to vacant benefices— some, like St. Laurence's Shaftesbury, denuded of its parson more than once, and one, Winterbourne St.

Nicholas, no less than three times. In a pastoral letter to his flock, he enjoined the sick to make confession to a layman if no priest was available and, if need be, to a woman. When the sacrament of Extreme Unction could not be administered, he concluded, 'faith must, as in other matters, suffice.'

In the adjoining diocese of Winchester, comprising the counties of Hampshire and Surrey which, by some miracle, escaped the infection almost till Christmas, Bishop Edington ordered the cathedral chapter to say the seven penitential and fifteen gradual psalms twice weekly and on Fridays to lead a procession of the clergy and people through the streets and market place, bare-footed and with bowed head, 'whilst with pious hearts they repeat their prayers and, putting away vain conversation, say as often as possible the Lord's Prayer and Hail Mary.' News most grave, he declared, had reached him; the cruel plague which had turned the cities of Europe into 'dens of wild beasts' had 'begun to afflict the coasts of the realm of England.' Towns, castles, and villages had been 'stripped of their population by the pestilence, more cruel than any two-edged sword, and become abodes of horror . . . We are struck with the gravest fear lest, which God forbid, the fell disease ravage any part of our diocese.' Already it was spreading through that of Exeter, falling first, as everywhere, on the seaports and estuaries and then following the course of the rivers inland. The clergy and laity of Devon and Cornwall went down like corn before the reaper; at the Cistercian abbey of Newenham twenty monks and three lay brothers died and only the abbot and two others survived. At the Augustinian priory of Bodmin two canons alone lived to tell the tale; the abbots of Hartland, Tavistock, and

St. Nicholas Exeter all perished, the last house losing two heads in succession.

The plague reached London at the beginning of November—'about the feast of All Hallows'. It took the great financier, Sir Thomas Pulteney—four times Mayor and builder of the parish church of Little All Hallows, Thames Street—the Princess Joan of Kent's uncle, Lord Wake of Liddel, four wardens of the Goldsmiths' Company, and the abbot and twenty-six monks of Westminster. The adjoining hospital of St. James's was left without inmates, all the brethren and sisters perishing; perhaps, like the brave nuns of the Hôtel Dieu at Paris, 'tending the sick with all sweetness and humility, putting all fear behind their backs.' Of the Bishop of Rochester's household, four priests, five esquires, seven acolytes, six pages, and ten serving-men died. The courts of Kings Bench and Common Pleas came to a standstill; a Parliament, summoned for January, was prorogued indefinitely. All through the winter the pestilence raged in the rat-haunted streets and alleys until, having carried off nearly half the population, 'by the intervention of the grace of the Holy Spirit on Whit-Sunday it ceased.' 'The cemeteries', a chronicler wrote, 'were not big enough and fields had to be set aside for the burying of the dead . . . Men and women bore their own offspring on their shoulders to the church and cast them into the common pit, from which there proceeded so great a stench that hardly anyone dared to cross.' A croft near Smithfield given by the Bishop of London for the burial of the dead became known as Pardon church yard; another just outside the north wall of the city bought by the defender of Aiguillon, Sir Walter Manny, was endowed with a Carthusian cell which was to become the site of the Charterhouse and the great London school which still bears its name.

Owing to the speed with which the plague slew, the worst was over in the south before it struck the midlands and north. By the spring of 1349 it had reached Norfolk. In Acle church a contemporary Latin inscription relates how that summer 'the brute beast plague' raged 'hour by hour'; the Norwich Dominicans died to a man. At Haveringland every member of the priory perished; in the little manor of Cornard Parva twenty-one families disappeared altogether. At Old Hunstanton 172 tenants of the manor died, 74 of them leaving no male heirs and 19 no single blood relation. Here, as in other places, if once a household was attacked, the tendency was for all to go. The midlands suffered almost as severely; the Leicester chronicler recorded that in the small parish of St. Leonard's 380 perished, in that of Holy Cross 400, in St. Margaret's 700. At Oxford, where the schools were closed for lack of students, two mayors died within a month.

Before the summer ended the plague had crossed the Humber. In the West Riding the incumbents of nearly half its parishes died; in the East Riding almost as many. The great Cistercian abbey of Meaux in Holderness lost its abbot and all but ten of forty-two monks and seven lay brethren; Fountains was so reduced that one of the twin fireplaces in the calefactorium where the quarterly bleedings took place was permanently bricked up. Scotland, protected by a hundred miles of moorland, escaped until the end of the year. At first the Scots ascribed the affliction of their neighbours to their wickedness, swearing 'by the foul death of England' and congratulating themselves on their own immunity. But when they gathered in Selkirk forest to harry the border, 'their joy turned to mourning as the sword of the wrath of God ... scourged them in fury and suddeness, smiting them not less than the English with abscesses and pustules.' Next year it was the turn of the Welsh mountain valleys, and 'at last, as if sailing thither, the plague reached Ireland, striking down great numbers of the English dwelling there' and wrecking the precarious framework of the manorial system of the Pale. 'It scarcely touched the pure Irish who dwelt in the mountains and upland areas until 1357, when it unexpectedly destroyed them far and wide in terrible fashion.' For the Black Death spared neither nation nor creed but inflicted misery on ever-widening circles of humanity. After it had devastated the rich cities of the Rhineland, multitudes of Jews, driven from their homes by superstitious and murderous mobs, fled eastwards across Europe to the Polish plains where an enlightened king, less cruel than his fellow Christians, offered them refuge.

Though the Black Death visited every part of England its incidence was uneven. Some villages like Tilgarsley in Oxfordshire and Middle Carlton and Ambion in Leicestershire—site of the future battle of Bosworth Field—were so depopulated that they were never reoccupied. Other places seem to have escaped almost unscathed. At St. Albans the abbot, prior, sub-prior, and forty-six monks died; at Christ Church, Canterbury, only four. Those who suffered most were the poor in their overcrowded hovels, and the parish and regular clergy. The nobility, living in comparatively clean and spacious conditions, escaped lightly; in England at least they had had plenty of warning of danger. Isolating themselves in some retired country place and keeping a strict guard against strangers, they let the pestilence pass them by. A few caught the infection; three archbishops of Canterbury died in that terrible year, one of them, John Stratford, at the end of August 1348 possibly from natural causes, but the other two of plague. The rest of the episcopal bench, immured in their country manor-houses, escaped, though Gynwell of Lincoln, true to his diocese's great tradition, toured his eight counties throughout the epidemic as usual. Of the parish clergy at least forty per cent died, most of them probably at their posts, though to remain must have been certain death. Others, we know from contemporary testimony, succumbed to the general panic and fled. The episcopal registers—better preserved and more complete in England than in any other country—suggest that, including monks and friars, nearly half the personnel of the Church was taken.

Of the general public it is impossible to estimate with any certainty the proportion who died; the verdict of modern scholarship is that the first outbreak alone probably carried off about one in three of the population. Contemporary chroniclers and eye-witnesses believed the casualty-rate to be much higher. Thomas Walsingham of St. Albans reckoned 'well-nigh half of all mankind', and others as much as two-thirds or even three-quarters. As the authors of such first-hand accounts were mostly writing of places where the plague was fiercest and from which many of the inhabitants had already fled, the fatality-rate of those who remained may have been almost as high as they supposed. What is certain is that, once established in the soil, the plague remained endemic. Dormant for perhaps a dozen years it would suddenly flare up, first in one city, then in another, at least once in a generation. For three hundred years—a period of time as great as that which divides us from the last outbreak in Charles II's reign—the red cross on the stricken door, the cart piled with corpses on its way to the plague-pit, the cry of 'Bring out your dead!' formed a recurrent part of the background of English life. During the three centuries since the Norman Conquest the population of England had probably doubled. The generation born in the middle of Edward III's reign saw it halved.

It is hard to realise the impact of a cataclysm carrying off one in three, probably one in two, of a civilised community. Its immediate effect, and of the shock and terror which accompanied it, was chaos. In the dirt and squalor of medieval life men were used to epidemic disease, but this was no ordinary epidemic. While it continued all activity was suspended. The harvest could not be gathered, taxes or rents collected, markets held or justice done. At the Bishop of Durham's halmote court at Houghton on 14 July 1349 it was recorded that 'no one will pay the fine for any land which is in the lord's hands through fear of plague; and so all are in the same way of being proclaimed as defaulters until God shall bring some remedy.' Everywhere there were vacant holdings and unculti-vated farms, and for a time it was almost impossible to sell anything. In the Leicester chronicler's words, 'everything was low in price because of the fear of death, for few took care of riches or property of any kind. A man could have a horse that had been worth 40s. for half a mark, a fat ox for 4s., a cow for 12d., a heifer for 6d., a fat wether for 4d., a sheep for 3d., a lamb for 2d., a large pig for 5d., a stone of wool for 9d.

Sheep and cattle ran loose through the fields and among the crops, and there was none to drive them off or herd them; for lack of care they perished in ditches and hedges in incalculable numbers.' To aggravate matters, a murrain, popularly attributed to the infection of the air, carried off vast numbers of livestock; in one Leicestershire pasture alone more than 5,000 sheep perished, 'so putrid that neither beast nor bird would touch them.'

Indeed, to some, the immediate aftermath of the Black Death seemed almost as ominous as the plague itself. 'Only the dregs of the people survive', an unknown hand inscribed on a stone of Ashwell church against the date 1349. 'Throughout the whole of that winter and spring,' wrote a Rochester monk, 'the bishop, an old and decrepit man, remained at Trotterscliff, saddened and grieving over the sudden change of the age. And in every manor of the bishopric buildings and walls fell to ruins. In the monastery there was such a scarcity of provisions that the community was troubled with great want of food, so much so that the monks were obliged to grind their own bread.' When the bishop visited the abbeys of Malling and Lesnes he found them so poor 'that, as is thought, from the present age to the day of Judgement they can never recover.'

Nor did the pestilence have the purging effect hoped for by moralists of making the survivors work harder and become more charitable to one another. A few serious Christians were stimulated to good works and greater thoughtfulness, like that imaginative warrior, Henry of Lancaster, the conqueror of Guienne, who not only endowed a collegiate church at Leicester but, after going on a crusade against the Baltic pagans, wrote in 1354 a long devotional treatise entitled *Le Livre de Seyntz Medicines*—an allegory of self-condemnation, 'written', as he put it, 'by a foolish wretched sinner who calls himself Henry duke of Lancaster—may God pardon his misdeeds.' But the world as a whole was not changed for the better. 'People', as a French chronicler wrote, 'were afterwards more avaricious and grasping, even when they possessed more of the goods of this world than before. They were more covetous, vexing themselves by contentious quarrels, strifes and law-suits . . . Charity, too, began to grow cold, and wickedness with its attendant, ignorance, was rampant, and few were found who would or could teach children the rudiments of grammar.' The Rochester monk, William Dene, tells the same story:

> The people for the greater part ever became more depraved, more prone to every vice and more inclined than before to evil and wickedness, not thinking of death nor of the past plague nor of their own salvation . . . Priests, little weighing the sacrifice of a contrite spirit, betook themselves to where they could get larger stipends than in their own benefices, on which account many benefices remained unserved. Day by day, the dangers to soul both in clergy and people multiplied . . . The labourers and skilled workmen were imbued with such a spirit of rebellion that neither king, law nor justice could curb them.

Twice in the twenty years after its first outbreak, and a third time before the end of the century, the Black Death returned. In the autumn of 1361 it broke out again and, before it ceased in the following May, had struck down the flower of another generation. This

time it was less discriminating, carrying off three of the
war heroes—'the good duke' of Lancaster, the earl of
Hereford, and Lord Cobham—and four bishops,
including that of London. It fell with particular
severity on children; *la mortalité des enfants* it was
called to distinguish it from its predecessors. While it
was raging, on 15 January 1362, a terrible tempest also
struck the country. 'Wretched, savage and violent', an
unknown writer recorded on the wall of Ashwell
church, 'a wicked populace survives to witness, and in
the end with a violent wind Maurus thunders in the
world.'

Seven years later, in the spring of 1369, the Black
Death returned for the third time in a generation.
Among those who died was the heroine of Chaucer's
poem, the *Book of the Duchess*—daughter and co-
heiress of the warrior duke of Lancaster who had
perished in the previous outbreak and wife of Edward
III's fourth son, John of Gaunt, who inherited through
her the four earldoms of Lancaster, Derby, Lincoln,
and Leicester, and, with them, the greatest fortune in
England. 'Glad she was, fresh and sportive, sweet,
simple and humble semblance, the fair lady whom men
called Blanche', wrote Froissart. Two years before her
death of the plague she had borne her husband a son,
named after the castle of his birth, Bolingbroke. Thirty
years later he was to lead a rebellion against his
autocratic cousin, Richard II, and receive from
Parliament an usurped crown on the grounds that
Richard had broken the fundamental laws of the
kingdom. By that time all the vast overseas conquests
of England had been lost save Calais. To the men of that
age the Black Death, the dethronement of the King,
and the defeat of their formerly victorious armies

seemed alike a judgement from God, proving, in the poet Langland's words, that

> These pestilences were purely for sin,
> And the south-west wind at Saturday at even
> Were plainly for pure pride and for no point else . . .
> In example for men that they should do better.

4

The Vision of Piers Plowman

For one Piers Plowman hath impugned us all
And set all sciences at naught save love alone.

William Langland

THE EFFECT OF THE BLACK DEATH on the nation's religious life was grave and prolonged. Of the regular and beneficed clergy something like half had perished. Reduced to penury by the reduced size of their congregations, the incumbents of many of the poorer benefices threw up their livings and sought more profitable employment as chantry-clerks or chaplains. In the words of William Langland, himself a poor chantry-clerk,

Parsons and parish priests complained to the bishop
That their parishes were poor since the pestilence time,
And asked leave and licence in London to dwell,
And sing *requiems* for stipends for silver is sweet.

The problem facing England at the end of Edward III's reign was a moral one. A succession of inexplicable disasters had befallen her; defeat in war, the loss of her conquests, the death of the Black Prince, heir to the throne. The harvests had failed, wool-prices had slumped, the Black Death had returned three times.

The nation's rulers were accusing one another of treason and malversation of public funds, and, for all the display of wealth in high places, the poor groaned under unjust taxation.

There could be only one explanation. The kingdom had outraged the laws of God and was suffering retribution. For medieval man believed that divine justice ruled the universe and that sooner or later every breach of it would be automatically punished. The thought of it haunted everyone, from the King on his throne to the peasant in the fields. The very brutes in the stinking city alsatias, the outlaws in the woods, the *routiers* as they murdered, burnt, and raped in pursuit of their merciless profession, could not escape its insistent, disturbing reminders.

God had ordained men to live in harmony with a divine order; the task of those who ruled was to see that order observed. The King's function as supreme judge rested on this belief; his judges, though no longer ecclesiastics, wore, as they still do, the churchman's gown. When the Commons debated the state of the kingdom in Parliament they sat in the chapter house of Westminster Abbey like monks in a circle while each speaker began his speech from the lectern with the words, *Jube Domine benedicere*—'Lord let Thy blessing'—and ended it with the equally familiar liturgical phrase, *Tu, autem, Domine, miserere nobis*—'Thou, Lord, have mercy on us'. And when the Speaker assumed his charge he declared it to be 'out of reverence to God'.

To define justice—*justicia* or righteousness— medieval man looked to the Church. Yet though the Church existed to teach men how to live justly, it was all too apparent that this was what so many of its

ministers failed to do themselves. For in the quarter of a
century following the coming of the Black Death there
had grown up a widespread feeling that the Church was
failing Christ's people. Bishops had come to seem
proud luxurious lords; archdeacons and proctors,
blackmailers; monks gluttons; friars scroungers and
liars. The Caesarian prelates, who helped the King
govern and administer the realm, in particular came in
for attack. 'They leave their flocks and spend their days
in the courts of the mighty to eat the flesh of fat beasts,'
thundered the great Dominican preacher, Dr Brom-
yard. Another sermon described them as living in
'strong castles and manors as royal as the King himself',
surrounded by knights, squires, yeomen, and grooms,
as they sat at their meat 'with precious vessels and royal
cupboards of silver and gold, and their men falling
down as to a god at every draught they drink.' When
one of them rode out,

> yea, though it be to visit his poor sheep, he must ride
> with four or five score horse, proudly apparelled at all
> points, his own palfrey worth twenty or thirty pounds
> all behanged with glittering gold as though it were an
> holy horse, himself above in fine scarlet or other cloth
> as good, and within as good a pelure as the Queen hath
> in any of her gowns; his parsons and clerks riding
> about him, all in gilt harness with swords overgilt
> hanging by their sides as though it were Centurio and
> his knights riding towards Christ's death.

Yet Christ himself, the preacher recalled, had no house
to cover his head and no ménage but 'twelve silly poor
men whom he served oftener than ever they served
him.' It was this contrast which caused Fitzralph of
Armagh to denounce his fellow prelates 'as plunderers,
thieves, and robbers, who seize the fruits of churches

and despise the sacred service of them; who are always exercising the cry, "Shear! shear!" and never fulfil the command, "Feed! feed!" '

This, though it represented a widely held view, was unjust, for many of Edward III's bishops were great public benefactors as well as able and hard-working administrators. William Edington of Winchester, who from an obscure origin rose to be successively Treasurer and Chancellor, rebuilt the presbytery of his cathedral in the new Perpendicular style partly at his own expense and endowed his native village in Wiltshire with a superb collegiate church. His successor, William of Wykeham, son of a small Hampshire freeholder, used the endowments of his see and the many benefices he held in plurality to continue the rebuilding of the cathedral and to found, first, New College, Oxford, and then his great school at Winchester, in order to make good the wastage in the ranks of the clergy caused by the Black Death. Contemptuously described by Wycliffe as 'a clerk wise in building castles and worldly doings' and the greatest pluralist of his day, he was nonetheless a generous and kindly man who faced misfortune when it came to him with philosophy and who used his power with moderation and humility. Bishop Richard Bury of Durham, another of Edward III's Chancellors, was a bibliophile who corresponded with Petrarch, founded a famous library and wrote a handbook on its use, called the *Philobiblon*, extolling the delights of reading. The most famous scholar of them all was the saintly Thomas Bradwardine—*doctor profundus*—mathematician, astronomer, philosopher, and theologian—the humble-hearted Merton fellow who had been the King's confessor at Crécy and, called to the primacy after two

Archbishops of Canterbury had died in the year of the first Black Death, hurried to England only to perish of the pestilence within a week of receiving the temporalities of his see. His successor, Simon Islip, though a comparatively poor man, founded an Oxford college for monks, while his successor, Simon Sudbury, set in hand the work of rebuilding the nave of Canterbury and laid the foundations of its present glory. Grandisson of Exeter, a princely patron of art, completed the nave of the West Country cathedral and added the musicians' gallery.

Yet all their learning, munificence, and industry in the service of the Crown availed the statesmen-prelates nothing. Their excessive wealth condemned them. Even a saint like Brunton of Rochester—the Norwich Benedictine and Balliol fellow who was probably 'the angel of Heaven' who 'loved to speak in Latin' mentioned in Langland's *Piers Plowman*—could not hope to bridge the gulf which divided such lordly hierarchs from ordinary mortals. As for the papacy, to which before England and her rulers had been so loyal, it was even more fatally damned in the eyes of humble Englishmen by its wealth and the rapacity with which it pursued it. To provide for its luxurious court at Avignon and swollen bureaucracy it employed the techniques of the lawyer, tax-collector, and money-lender, extending its grip on the ecclesiastical benefices and endowments of every country in Christendom. In the eyes of those who were coming to think of themselves as Englishmen, the papacy no longer seemed the protector but the exploiter of the *Ecclesia Anglicana*.

In place of the apostolic and intellectual ferments of the twelfth and thirteenth centuries the papal problems of the fourteenth centred round ecclesiastical taxation, first-fruits, provisions to benefices, and the sale of pardons and indulgences. Annates—part of the first year's revenue of a benefice—were demanded of all new incumbents, the ready cash to pay being advanced to them by the papal bankers at usurious interest-rates which were subsequently enforced—in disregard of the Christian prohibition against usury—by threats of excommunication. No papel debt, it was said, was ever remitted. And, because of the French war and the papal residence at Avignon, the Pope's canonical right to appoint to benefices was increasingly resented by an England which had become insular and self-sufficient. In 1376 the knights and burgesses of the 'good' Parliament presented a petition to the King and Council complaining that 'the court of Rome, which ought to be the fountain, root and source of holiness and destruction of covetousness, simony, and other sins,' had attracted to itself the collation of so many 'bishoprics, dignities, prebendaries and other benefices of Holy Church in England' that it was drawing from the country more than five times as much as the total royal revenue from taxation. This was a gross exaggeration, but it showed how far popular feeling had been exacerbated by papal practices. Other items in the Commons' complaint were that bishops were so heavily indebted to the curia for the fees and first-fruits of their benefices that they were forced to cut down their woods, borrow from their friends, and demand crushing aids and subsidies from their tenants and diocesan clergy; that, as a result of simony by 'brokers of benefices who dwell in the sinful city of Avignon,' 'a miserable fellow who knows nothing and is worth nothing' would be advanced to an incumbency worth a thousand marks, while an English doctor or a master of divinity had to content himself with a fiftieth of that amount, 'so that clerks lose hope of preferment by their orders and talent for learning . . . and people are ceasing to send their children to school, and the clergy, who are the substance of Holy Church and our holy Faith, fall into decline and annihilation.'

So unpopular had the papacy become with the English that when, just before little King Richard's accession, the city of London put on a pageant in his honour 'with great noise of minstrelsy, trumpets, cornets and shawms and many wax torches', the highlight in the procession was a mock Pope accompanied by twenty-four cardinals and 'eight or ten arrayed with black masks like devils, not at all amiable, seeming like Legates.' When, following an attempt to re-establish the papacy at Rome, the French cardinals in 1378 challenged the election of a fantastically irascible and autocratic Italian Pope, Urban VI, on grounds of intimidation by the Roman mob, and set up with the help of his enemies a rival one at Avignon under the name of Clement VII, an English Parliament decided to support Urban and, by doing so, helped to perpetuate for the next half century an even greater scandal than the seventy years' Babylonish captivity—the simultaneous existence of two and, at one time, three Popes. Each Pope demanded the payment of ecclesiastical taxes and each excommunicated the other as anti-Christ, while both declared a crusade and hired the terrible roving bands which had been left over from the Anglo-French wars to devastate the lands and massacre the supporters of the other. The 'seamless robe of Christ', as a preacher put it, was rent asunder, and, to the horror and bewilderment of simple Christians,

Urbanists and Clementists fought one another for His garments.

The man who saw furthest into the Christian predicament was not a philosopher or ecclesiastical dignitary but a poor chantry-clerk in minor orders, earning a precarious living saying masses for men's souls. Born, it is believed, about 1330 in the village of Colwall near Malvern, the illegitimate child of a peasant girl and an Oxfordshire gentleman named de Rokayle, William Langland was probably educated at the priory choir-school of Great Malvern and ordained as an acolyte in the winter of the first Black Death, subsequently drifting to London. Almost a generation before the Yorkshire scholar and theologian, John Wycliffe—Master of the little Oxford college of Balliol—acting under the powerful patronage of John of Gaunt, duke of Lancaster, uncle of the boy King Richard II, launched his famous attack on the wealth and worldliness of the Church, at the time of the second visitation of the plague in 1361/2, Langland wrote, in the alliterative metre and south Midland dialect of his Anglo-Saxon forbears, a poem called 'The Vision of William concerning Piers the Plowman'. Expanded fifteen years later during the revolutionary crisis between the death of the Black Prince in 1376 and that of the old King in the following year, and revised at least once before the poet's death towards the end of the century, it consisted of a series of allegorical visions in which, before the background of contemporary England, he sought for the secret of the Christian life.

Starting as a moral satire of the kind then common both in sermon and verse, it opened, far from the roar of Cheapside, in the land of the poet's boyhood

in a summer season when soft was the sunlight
. . . on a May morning on Malvern hills.

Resting under a bank beside a brook, he saw across the
Severn valley, outlined against the distant Cotswold
edge, the tower of Truth and beneath it a dungeon
surrounded by ditches, 'dark and dreadful of sight'.
Between him and these types of Heaven and Hell lay a
'fair field full of folk'

> of all manner of men the mean and the rich,
> Working and wandering as the world asketh.

There passed before him the King and his knights and
'the might of the community', barons and burgesses,
mayors and mace-bearers 'that act as a mean between
King and Commons in keeping the law'; lovely ladies
whose long fingers had silks and satins to sew at leisure
to 'make chasubles for chaplains in honour of the
churches'; serjeants-at-law hovering like hawks in
silken hoods and 'pleading at law for pounds and
pennies'; 'merchants—proud-hearted men, patient of
tongue'

> buxom in their bearing to burgesses and lords,
> But to poor people having pepper in the nose

Bakers, brewers, and butchers, weavers of wool and of
linen, tailors, tinkers, and tax-collectors; 'Peter the
pardoner, Bertie the beadle of Buckinghamshire,
Reginald the reeve of Rutland and Mumps the miller',
all were there.

Some were putting out to plough, had little play-time,
In setting seed and sowing, sweated at their labour,
Winning wealth that the worthless wasted in gluttony.
Some pranked themselves in pride preciously apparelled,

Coming under colour of costly clothing . . .
Beggars and blackguards went busily about
With their bellies and bags all brimming with bread,
Feigning sick for food and fighting in the ale-house . . .
Cissy the sempstress sat on a bench,
Robin the rabbit-catcher and his wife with him,
Tim the tinker and two of his apprentices,
Hickey the hackney-man and Hodge the huckster,
Clarice of Cock's Lane and the clerk of the parish,
Parson Peter Proudie and his Peronella,
Davy the ditcher and a dozen others.
A fiddler, a rat-catcher, a Cheapside crossing-sweeper,
A rope-maker, a road-man and Rosy the dishwasher,
Godfrey of Garlick-hithe and Griffin the Welshman . . .
Jack the juggler and Janet of the stews,
Daniel the dice-player and Denis the bawd.*

Mingling with them the poet saw his fellow-churchmen. There was Sloth the parson who could neither sing nor read but could find a hare in a field or furrow better than a *beatus*; 'curates under Christ with the tonsure for token' who lodged 'lazily in London all the year round' or served the King, 'counting his silver in Exchequer and Chancery'; monks who had no pity on the poor, 'though money rained on their altars'; university doctors 'putting forth assumptions to prove the truth' and 'gnawing God with their gorge' while they dined on the dais on delicate dishes

> And the cry of the care-stricken calls at their gate,
> The hungry and thirsty that quake for cold,
> With none to take them in and tend their suffering.

The Vision of Piers Plowman, translated into modern English by Nevill Coghill. Where otherwise not stated the transcriptions, with the spelling modernised, are partly my own, based on the text of Dr Skeat and the admirable modern version of Donald and Rachel Attwater in the Everyman's Library edition.

There were friars

all the four Orders,
Preaching the people for their private profit,
Glossing the gospel as seemed good to them;

pardoners pulling out briefs with bishops' seals to
cozen poor folk for their gold; hermits with hooked
staves on the road to Walsingham, 'their wenches with
them'; 'long lousy lubbers that were loth to labour',
and squabbling nuns in convents with Wrath as cook,
making

a pottage or prattling that Dame Joan was a bastard,
And Dame Clarice a knight's daughter and her father a
cuckold;
Dame Peronelle a priest's wench that could never be
prioress,
For she had a child in cherry-time all the chapter knew it.

Bishops and bachelors, chancellors and masters, deans,
archdeacons, and registrars, 'saddled with silver our
sins to sanction', the whole personnel of the Church in
England passed before the poet's eyes.

Langland saw that what was true of the laity was true
of the clergy.

The most part of this people that passeth on earth
Have worship in this world and wish for no better.

Both were corrupted by the universal craving for
worldly reward; both had forgotten the purpose of
Christianity. It was from the true Church, as he
encountered her in his dream, that he rediscovered
what that end was:

Truth telleth that love is the governance* of Heaven.

* Langland's actual word was triarchy (Skeat gives 'triacle')—the rule of
the Trinity.

... The Father that formed us all
Looked on us with love and let his Son die
Meekly for our misdeeds to amend us all ...
Yet meekly with his mouth Mercy he besought
To have pity on that people that pained him to death ...
Therefore I warn you rich to have pity on the poor,
Though ye be mighty in power be meek in your works
For the same measures that ye mete to others
Ye shall be weighed therewith when ye wend hence ...
Unless you love liberally and lend to the poor
Of such goods as God sends gladly them giving,
Ye have no more merit in mass nor in hours
Than Malkyn of her maidenhood that no man desires.

Turning their backs on the world, the dreamer and a
crowd of penitents set off on pilgrimage to find St.
Truth—a saint whom a professional palmer, his hat and
cloak covered with tokens of the shrines he had visited,
assured them he had never heard of. It was at this point
that the pilgrims encountered by the roadside a poor
labouring ploughman whose simple faith in God and
unseeking service to his fellow men stood out in
contrast to the shams and vanities of Church and State.
Because, uncomplaining, he bore the burden of others,
because he was truthful, just and faithful to his word
and spent his days tilling and toiling for the common
profit 'as a true life asks', he was able to point the way
to St. Truth. 'Look to the deed', he told the pilgrims

that thy word declareth,
Such as thou seemest at sight be in the trial found.

His was an old-fashioned morality. He expected
knights and lords to protect Holy Church and guard
the husbandman from wasters and robbers, to hunt the
game that damaged hedges and crops, to be merciful to
poor tenants and refrain from taxing them unjustly. He

denounced idlers, beggars, and ribalds and all who lived irregular lives. 'Robert the runabout', he declared, 'shall have naught of mine.'

For Langland had no more liking for a needy rogue and idler than for a rich one. His father had been a vassal of the ancient Marcher house of Despenser and, for all his poverty, he seems to have inherited a respect for the feudal loyalties. He had no wish to overturn the polity in which he lived, only to make it more just. When in his poem a knight, his conscience touched by Piers's example of sacrifice and honesty, asked him what was his duty,

'By St. Paul,' quoth Perkin, 'ye proffer you so fair
That I shall swynk and sweat and sow for us both,
And other labours do for thy love all my lifetime,
In covenant that thou keep Holy Church and myself
From wasters and from wicked men that this world
    destroyeth.'

There was no hate in this conservative moralist's creed, only a longing for justice. 'Christ on his Cross', he wrote, 'made us all blood-brethren.'

Yet the contrast between ill-used wealth and undeserved and unrelieved destitution shocked Langland deeply. To him, as to later English idealists, it seemed a denial of Christianity that the honest poor should be oppressed and defrauded. It was an outrage against the founder of his religion.

Jesu Christ of heaven
In a poor man's apparel pursueth us ever . . .
For on Calvary of Christ's blood Christendom gan spring,
And brethren in blood we become there . . . and gentlemen
    each one.

Langland's heart was stirred and his indignation roused

for 'prisoners in pits and poor folk in cottages, charged with children and chief lord's rent':

> Old men and hoary without help or strength,
> And all women with child that can work no more,
> The blind and bedridden and broken in limb,
> That bears mischief meekly as lepers and others; . . .
> For love of their lowly hearts our Lord hath granted
> Their penance and purgatory here on this earth.

While they were neglected, he could not reverence 'lords and ladies and persons in fur and silver'. At the back of his vision lay always the memory of the Cross and of all that Christ had suffered in poverty and obscurity, that men might have life and have it more abundantly.

> I fell once more asleep and suddenly me met
> That Piers the Plowman was painted all bloody
> And come in with a cross before the common people,
> And right like in all limbs to our Lord Jesu.
> Then called I Conscience to ken me the truth.
> 'Is this Jesus the jouster,' quoth I, 'that Jews did to death?
> Or is it Piers the Plowman? Who painted him so red?'
> Quoth Conscience and kneeled: 'These are Piers's arms,
> His colours and coat-armour and he that cometh so bloody
> Is Christ with his cross conqueror of Christendom.'

It was a very different heraldry to that of the knights of the Garter feasting in the Round Tower at Windsor.

Stronger even than Langland's longing for justice was his sense of compassion. When idlers and wasters shirked their work in Piers's field and, as a result, were scourged by Hunger, the ploughman had pity of them and fed them, though he knew that, once the famine had passed, they would fall to their idle ways again.

They're my brethren by blood, for God bought us all.
Truth taught me once to love them each one
And to help them in all things always as they need . . .
Love them and loathe them not; let God take the
    vengeance.

The work, not of a highly educated man protected by
inherited wealth from the harsh animal struggle and
squalid barbarism of medieval poverty but of one living
precariously on its fringe, *Piers Plowman* faces the full
Christian challenge. It is far more than a protest against
social injustice, though none more eloquent has ever
been written. It is a profound religious poem—as
remarkable in its content, if not in its literary form, as
the *Divine Comedy*. For all his asceticism, the virtues
its author prized were mercy and charity. When a priest
read out a pardon which Piers had secured from Truth
for all who had worked on earth honestly or suffered
unmerited hardship or poverty, and it was found to
contain only the harsh words, 'Do well and have well
and God shall have thy soul. Do evil and have evil and
after thy death the Devil shall have thy soul; hope thou
none other', the ploughman hero, confronted by this
unrelenting piece of Old Testament justice, indignantly
tore it up.

For when, after awakening, 'meatless and money-
less', on Malvern hills, the poet once more renewed his
visionary quest of the Christian mystery, roaming
alone 'all a summer season', it was to discover
something that transcended the standards of 'Do-
Well', exemplar of the stern saving virtues on which the
priest had insisted. Halted by the 'bliss of the birds'
singing 'by a woodside in a wild wilderness' and
leaning under a linden 'to listen to the lay of these
lovely fowl', he fell into a dream in which a tall man,

like to himself, called him by his name and revealed himself as Thought. From him he found the answer he was seeking.

'Do-well and Do-better and Do-best,' quoth he
'Are three fair virtues and be not far to find.
Whoso is true of his tongue and of his two hands,
And through his labour or through his land his livelihood
    winneth,
And is trusty of his tallying, taketh but his own,
And is not a drunkard or disdainful, Do-well him
    followeth.

'Do-better doth right thus and he doth much more,
He is lowly as a lamb and loving of speech
And helpeth all men as they needeth . . .

'Do-best is above both and beareth a bishop's cross,
It is hooked at one end to hale men from Hell:
A pike is on that staff to pull down the wicked.'

Throughout the rest of the poem, most English in its lack of logical order, its whimsical incongruity, and underlying strength of feeling, the poet is guided by allegorical characters to comprehend each of the three ascending types in the scale of Christian perfection. Of each Piers, like Christ in his life on earth, becomes the prototype, first in his original form representing

all living labourers that live by their hands
And take the just wages they honestly earn
And live in love and law,

—a type that comprised for Langland all, in whatever walk of life, who did their duty by their fellow-men. With Do-better the poem passed from the Old Testament to the New. Its essence is love:

He bids us be as brethren and pray for our enemies,
And love them that lie to us and help them when need help
And do good against evil for God himself commands it.

The virtues now demanded are mercy, forgiveness,
patience in affliction and poverty, cheerful acceptance
of whatever God sends. Men should take no thought
for the morrow but, loving their fellows, learn from
nature how Providence provides for all in its 'kind',
how 'lent never was life but livelihood was given'—a
theme which enables the poet to reveal his passionate
love of nature:

I saw the sun and the sea and the sands after
And where the birds and beasts seek after their mates,
Wild worms in the woods and wonderful birds
With flecked feathers and of many colours.

Piers has now embraced the life of contemplation—one
that made a strong appeal to a poor unbeneficed scholar
like Langland—

For if heaven be on this earth and ease to any soul,
It is in cloister or in learning . . .;
For in cloister cometh no man to chide or fight,
For all is courtesy there and book to read and to learn

—a passage followed by his scathing indictment of
what cloistered life had become in contemporary
England. As Do-better, his hero's way of life follows
the path of full Christian charity wherever it leads.
'Whoso giveth not, loveth not', is his creed; there is no
limit to its practical expression.

Jesus Christ of Heaven
In a poor man's apparel pursueth us ever
And looketh on us in their likeness and that with lovely
cheer
To know us by our kind hearts.

81

In the final stages of his dream the poet encounters the supreme form of Christian virtue:

> Do well, my friend, is to do as law teacheth,
> To love thy friend and thy foe that is Do-better.
> To give and to succour both young and old,
> To heal and to help is Do-best of all.

And suddenly we realise that Piers has become the prototype of Christ himself. We see him, as Do-best, riding into Jerusalem to do battle for man's soul:

> This Jesus of his gentlihood will joust in Piers's arms
> In his helm and in his hauberk *humana natura*.

There follows the most wonderful scene in the poem, the Harrowing of Hell, when, after the agony on the cross, the risen Christ challenges Lucifer in his dark realm and, heralded by Light, demands the souls of the damned:

> 'What lord art thou' quoth Lucifer, '*Quis est iste?*'
> '*Rex gloriae,*' the Light replied,
> 'And Lord of might and main and all manner of virtues.
> Dukes of this dim place, undo these gates
> That Christ may come in the King's son of Heaven!'

Then Piers, now God incarnate, himself speaks

> 'I that am lord of life love is my drink,
> And for that drink today I died upon earth . . .
> Now shall I come as a King, crowned with angels,
> And have out of Hell all men's souls, . . .
> For I were an unkind King unless I my kind helped.'

In his belief in the ultimate redemption of all men, even the damned, Langland went far beyond the Christian theology of his age. It was no academic reasoning that had brought him to this conclusion but his knowledge of mankind's inherent sinfulness and desperate need for forgiveness and regeneration, and his unshakable faith in Christ's all-embracing mercy.

So, as the Easter bells pealed out from London's steeples, the poet awoke—

> And called Kit my wife and Calotte my daughter—
> 'Arise and reverence God's resurrection,
> And creep to the cross on thy knees and kiss it for a jewel,
> For God's blessed body it bore for our salvation.'

Langland's vision of Christianity was a purely personal one. He saw that the Faith depended not merely on conformity to the Church's creed and ritual—in which no man believed more firmly than he—but on the individual's pursuit of truth and his performance of acts of Christian love. It rested not merely on commemoration of Christ's sacrifice but on man's readiness to follow in His footsteps. 'Clerics have told me', he wrote,

> that Christ is in all places,
> Yet I never saw Him for certain save as myself in a mirror.

Piers Plowman is a restatement of a mystery incarnate: that the kindgom of Heaven is within everyone's reach, yet can only be won by love and sacrifice.

In the closing stanzas of his work revised before his death—no one knows exactly when he died or where he lies—appalled by the schism in Christendom and seeing Piers as the Peter to whom Christ had entrusted his Church, Langland made a passionate appeal for Christian unity:

> Cry we to the Commons that they come to unity
> And there abide and do battle against Belial's children.

Despite his realisation of his fellow-churchmen's failings, from his lowly station among the ecclesiastical

army's flotsam and jetsam he realised, as his great
contemporary, Wycliffe, failed to realise, mankind's
need for the Church's guidance, 'for Clergy is keeper
under Christ of Heaven'. His final word was of refusal
to despair and of his faith that somehow, notwithstand-
ing the universal corruption and disintegration of his
time, the search for truth and the Christian virtues
would in the end triumph.

> 'By Christ,' quoth Conscience then, 'I will become a
> pilgrim
> And walk as wide as the world lasteth
> To seek Piers the Plowman that Pride may destroy.'

In the all-embracing charity of this humble chantry-
clerk in the wake of a great national disaster lay a reflection of what, in the slow course of centuries, was
to become, at its best, the enduring spirit of England.

PART TWO
THE
LIVING PAST

5

Shakespeare's England

At length they all to merry London came . . .
. . . Sweet Thames, run softly till I end my song

Edmund Spenser

THE SHAKESPEARIAN CAPITAL from which, in the
opening decades of the seventeenth century, the first
American colonies sprang, was no old-fashioned town
inhabited by unadventurous backward-looking folk. It
was a fast expanding and intensely energetic, aggressive
and excitable community with only one foot in the
rustic England out of which it had sprung and the other
in the trading oceans. 'The most scoffing, respectless
and unthankful city that ever was', a contemporary
lover of the half clerical and monastic medieval London
of the past called it. It was peopled and ruled by men
who were the architects of their own fortunes and lived
by taking risks. They or their forefathers had taken a
very big one when they first migrated from the country
to the city to make their fortunes. For, out of every
three or four who came to London, at least two died of
plague or fever in its noisome, pestilential courts and
alleys. Their prototype was the fabulous Dick Whit-
tington, who according to popular legend had tramped
to London as a boy two centuries before with a cat and

all his wordly goods tied in a handkerchief on his back, and who, in real life, had lived to become Lord Mayor and the equivalent of a modern millionaire. It was such men, who, in the years following the defeat of the Armada, when Sheakespeare was writing his first plays, set the pace and found the finance for the feverish pioneering—the 'root, hog or die' courage—of the founding fathers of the United States.

Though in the Middle Ages England had been an island kingdom on the road to nowhere—the last outpost of civilised Christendom, save for wild Scotland and still wilder Ireland beyond it—during the reign of the Tudors, with the discovery of a new World beyond the Atlantic and of an ocean route round Africa to the golden East of silks and spices, she had gradually found herself in the commercial centre of the world instead of on its outer fringe. It had taken Londoners several generations to realise the full implications of this momentous change. But by the closing decades of Elizabeth's germinative reign, with the awareness of their national unity which she had awoken in them, its consciousness had given to the life of England's capital an immense vitality. When country lads—the Dick Whittingtons of the age—travelled to it, as thousands did every year, like young Will Shakespeare from Stratford-upon-Avon, hoping to make their fortunes in its crowded, narrow, evil-smelling, but intensely exciting streets, they felt that they were coming, not only to by far the largest city in their own island, but to the doorway to a greater and wider world.

It was this sense which pervaded the new plays of the Elizabethan and Jacobean dramatists, with their international settings and their plots taken from Athens and Rome, Sicily and Illyria, Denmark and Egypt, and the cities of Lombardy and Bohemia. It is a measure of Shakespeare's all-embracing genius that, while he peopled even the glades of Greece with Warwickshire rustics and first made his name as a dramatist by writing three chronicle plays immortalising the changing fortunes of the Lancastrian and Yorkist princes in the century before he was born, the themes and leading characters of his more ambitious comedies were scarcely ever taken from England, or if they were, were drawn from an England so remote in time as to be part of a foreign world. Even those of the great tragedies of his later years—the years when the first English settlers were about to make a lodgement beyond the Atlantic—Antony and great Caesar, Othello the Moor and Coriolanus, Timon of Athens and Hamlet the Dane, were not born within sound of Bow Bells or even those of Stratford-on-Avon.

This was the real significance of Shakespeare's London. It was English, but its face and bright eyes were turned toward the new lands of fable and romance beyond the seas. The Londoners of his day were as obsessed with the thought of those lands, of foreign princes and foreign courts and voyages to remote parts, as little boys today are with tales of flights to the moon. The rough mob which flocked to the new bear gardens, stews, and playhouses of Shoreditch and the South Bank were given dramas about merchants of Venice and gentlemen of Verona and Roman Caesars and senators because that was what they wanted to hear about. They might have burnt down the theatres—for they were not a patient or polite audience—had they been offered anything else.

One can see that vibrant city in John Stow's great *Survey of London*—written in the latter part of

Elizabeth's reign and published in 1598—a metropolis crowded and almost bursting at the seams with its fast-growing population: a proud, turbulent, beautiful, and dangerous city, with its filthy open ditches and rat-haunted laystalls and its crowded overhanging gabled houses almost touching one another across the narrow streets and inviting fire at the first spark. Such houses were framed in oak, with walls of lath and plaster, and their piled soaring stories painted and heavily carved. Because of the ever-present risk of fire, every substantial one had by law to keep a supply of leather fire-buckets, and every parish had its great iron hooks with ropes and pulleys for pulling down burning buildings.

Above the city towered the immense, five hundred-year-old St. Paul's Cathedral, the second largest in the world, crowned, until a few years after Elizabeth's accession, when it was struck in 1561 by lightning, by an enormous spire—150 feet higher than the dome and cross of its present successor. From the river Tudor London, with its forest of Gothic church spires and towers soaring above the little three-storied houses, must have made much the same impression on contemporaries as moden New York with its sky-scrapers seen from the sea. The city, among the largest in Europe, glimpsed from northern height or Kentish heath, gave the approaching traveller a breathtaking sense of size and urban sophistication, for it was far larger in proportion to all the other towns of the kingdom than it is today. Its population, a hundred thousand at the time of Elizabeth's accession in 1558 and a quarter of a million by the middle of the seventeenth century, was something like twenty times that of the next largest English city, Norwich. The noise and uproar—of hoofs and wheels on the cobbles, of apprentices and hawkers bawling their wares, of the constantly creaking painted and gilded signs which hung and swung over the narrow streets from every shop, inn, and alehouse—was like a cannonade.

Around the older and inner London of the Middle Ages the ancient walls still stood, thirty feet high in places, with bastions and gates such as King Hal had ridden through as he went out to Agincourt two centuries before. But the suburbs, or 'liberties' as they were called, with their rich merchants' pleasances and squalid squatters' hovels and shacks, were spreading their untidy tentacles in every direction over the fields. Within a lifetime of Shakespeare's death in 1616, despite the constant inroads of typhus and smallpox, and the horrifying epidemics of bubonic plague, which, until the last great pestilence in 1665, swept the city in almost every decade, 'this great and monstrous thing called London' stretched almost from Blackwall to Chelsea, as the twin cities of London and Westminster drew ever closer to one another. It was hard to say exactly where one entered it, but the traveller knew by the old formula, 'so soon as the coach was got upon the stones.'

For it was then that the rattle began—of wooden and iron wheels rumbling on cobbles—of apprentices standing before every shop bawling, 'What d'ye lack?'—of hawkers crying, 'Hot fine oatcake', 'Lily-white vinegar', 'White-hearted cabbages', and 'Kitchen stuff, ha' you maids'; and, as the warm months drew on and rich folk wished themselves on their country estates, 'Cherry Ripe', 'Peas', and 'Fine strawberries'. There were costard-mongers—the forerunners of the Victorian and Edwardian costers—hawking apples;

old-clothes men and small-coals men with sacks of Newcastle cobbles on their backs; milkmaids intoning 'Any milk here?' as they rattled their pails; tinkers with loud 'Have you any brass pots, iron pots, skillets or frying pans to mend?' and mousetrap men with 'Buy a mousetrap, a mousetrap, or a tormentor for your fleas?' One sensed the context of these incitements to commerce by their music rather than their words; by the lilt and rhythm of: 'Here's fine herrings, eight a groat!', 'Come buy my Wellsfleet oysters, ho!', 'Come buy my whitings fine and new!' For the art of advertising was then vocal, not visual.

One not only heard London, one smelt it. The sanitation of the age was oriental in its simple grandeur, and its effects, comparatively innocuous in a country village, were appalling in a metropolis. Rivers of filth coursed down the centre of every street, and at the time of the emptying of slop-pails, the passer-by nearest the wall had cause to be grateful for the overhanging stories. Around the city stretched a halo of stinking, steaming laystalls, haunted by flies and kites, while in its denser quarters the graveyards, piled high above the surrounding ground, constantly repeopled themselves. The most cultured, however nice in their own tastes, were utterly innocent of public sanitary sense: one great lord in Stuart times installed a pump to drive the piled ordure from his cellar into the street. Drinking water, though a few of the larger houses enjoyed a piped supply, was hawked from door to door in large wooden vessels, broad at the bottom and narrow at the top, and filled from the conduits at the principal street corners.

The streets between the crowded buildings were narrow, cobbled with egg-shaped stones, with posts at the sides of the broader thoroughfares to protect pedestrians, and rendered fantastically crooked by the uneven frontage of the houses. Above them painted signs indicated to an illiterate age the addresses of their occupants—the 'Three Pigeons' in Great Queen's Street, or the 'Crooked Billet' 'over against Hill, the Quaker cook's, upon the Mall Bank, Westminster.' Behind the streets were courtyards and lanes giving access to others still narrower, and to the stables which housed the countless riding and draught-horses of the metropolis.

Carts, coaches, and sledges jammed the narrow streets, and traffic control tended to be a matter of vocal adjustment 'till the quarrel be decided whether six of your nobles sitting together shall stop and give way to as many barrels of beer.' Every nobleman's coach was preceded by footmen calling on the groundlings to make way for their master, a demand which draymen and drivers of hackney coaches had no hesitation in disputing. These last, which waited for their fares in ranks at street corners, were a post-Elizabethan innovation, and, despite the attempts of the Thames watermen to get them prohibited, multiplied rapidly throughout the seventeenth century. By its second half they had firmly established themselves as one of the principal institutions of London. To travel in them was to be involved in frequent turmoil. There were traffic blocks which lasted half an hour and set whole streets swearing and shouting; accidents when wheels came off or bolts broke, so that the horses went on while the unfortunate passengers remained stationary; Jehu-like incidents which left splashed and endangered pedestrians screaming with rage, or in narrow thoroughfares brought down the hanging wares from the hooks outside the shops. Even at night, while the city slept, the clamour of London persisted, the constable and his watch brawling with midnight revellers, the watchman's cry of 'Past one of the clock and a cold frosty windy morning!' and the sounds of cattle, pigs, and poultry which bespoke the agricultural undertakings hidden behind London's urban exterior.

In winter the principal streets were lit until ten or eleven at night by lanterns placed at regular intervals, and, less certainly, by householders who were expected, between the feasts of All Saints and Candlemas, to expose their light to the roadway. In summer a frugal age dispensed with artificial illumination altogether. More reliable were the link-boys who waited at every corner with torch and lantern to light travellers home. These poor urchins, recruited from the ragged homeless strays who lodged in doorways and disused penthouses, assailed the passer-by with cries of, 'Do you want light?' Grander citizens went out to supper with a servant carrying a lanthorn before them and so provided their own street lighting.

If there was not much light by night, there was plenty of smoke by day, particularly in the winter when that of thousands of wood or sea-coal fires rose into the damp air. Above the city hung a permanent pall of vapour from the furnaces of brewers, soap boilers, and dyers. This phenomenon, already a minor nuisance at the end of Elizabeth's reign, had become a major one half a century later. Evelyn, the most fastidious observer of his day, wrote indignantly of the 'horrid smoke which obscures our churches and makes our palaces look old, which fouls our clothes and corrupts the waters.' In winter this coal vapour sometimes descended on the streets in a blanket of fog so thick that 'horses ran against each other, carts against carts, coaches against coaches.'

Trade and manufacturers were expanding fast; London was above all a city of merchants, shopkeepers, artisans, and turbulent apprentices. Traders still congregated in particular districts; the goldsmiths in Cheapside—the city's broadest street and most fashionable shopping centre—the fishmongers in Bridge Street, mercers and haberdashers on London Bridge, pepperers and grocers in Bucklersbury, booksellers and stationers in St. Paul's churchyard, where they set up their stalls against the walls of the ancient cathedral and stocked their books in its vaults. The raw materials of trade reached Londoners through the great provision markets—meat from Hungerford and Queenhithe, fish and coal from Billingsgate, cloth from Blackwell Hall, herbs from Covent Garden and the Stocks Market, horses and livestock from Smithfield, and fish, butter, poultry, bacon, hides, and leather from Leadenhall.

The shops were small, consisting generally of the front downstairs room of the house in which the shopkeeper's family and apprentices lived and worked. But though the multiple shop was unknown, the bazaar was already flourishing by the time of Shakespeare's death in 1616. Great ladies with their husbands and 'servants'—as their cavaliers were called—flocked to the New Exchange in the Strand, which, with its row of shops along double galleries of black stone, conveniently adjacent to the new fashionable quarter of the town round Covent Garden, during the reigns of the first two Stuarts had begun to outdistance the nave of St. Paul's and the old Royal Exchange in Cornhill as popular marts. And in the latter were those elegant young women, the sempstresses and milliners of the Exchange, who, with their ogling eyes and pretty chirpings of 'Fine linens, sir, gloves or ribbons', made gentlemen customers buy more than they had intended, and, unless they have been maligned by their contemporaries, were sometimes not averse to selling their persons as well.

All this business required refreshment, and it was easily to be had by those with well-lined purses. Eating houses ranged from famous taverns like the 'Boar's Head' in Eastcheap, the 'Mermaid' and 'Mitre' in Bread Street and Mitre Court, and the 'Sun' in Fish Street, to little cookshops where one could feast on a chop of veal, bread and cheese and beer for a shilling, or buy a joint or sirloin of roast ready cooked for consumption at home.

> The gentry to the 'King's Head',
> The nobles to the 'Crown',
> The knight unto the 'Golden Fleece',
> And to the 'Plough' the clown.

A common mode of dining in a tavern was to take the 'ordinary' at the long table, each man contributing to the conversation and paying his 'club' or share. Places of purely liquid refreshment were innumerable; had one tried to count all the alehouses between the 'Hercules Pillars' by Hyde Park Gate and the 'Boatswain' in Wapping, one might have counted for ever. In these, with their red or green painted lattices, men of all classes congregated to drink and talk, as often as not about the political doings of their betters—much to the astonishment of foreigners, who could not accustom themselves to the way the English left their work at all hours of the day for this purpose.

For London was not only a trading but an intensely libertarian city. It had been so from time immemorial: a refuge from and a counterweight to the feudal order of the English countryside. From its rich aldermen and livery men to its rowdy apprentices all its people claimed a large measure of liberty and what to foreigners seemed outrageous political licence. The traditional cry of 'clubs' could quickly fill a street with 'truncheoners', as the growing hatred and fear of 'popery' intensified after the massacre of St. Bartholomew in 1572, the atrocious cruelty of the Spanish Inquisition to English seamen captured beyond the 'Line', and the Gunpowder Plot of 1605. Ready to mob anyone who outraged popular beliefs and prejudices by the least suspicion or appearance of popery, if anyone interfered in the name of authority, the City's 'brisk Protestant boys' would beat up with impunity the constables and aged infirm watchmen who formed the bulk of its only police force.

Yet, for all its noise and turbulence, London was still half rustic. The fields were never far away, and most of the main streets filled at least once a day with herds of cattle and flocks of sheep, making their dolorous way to the markets which fed London's swarming population. Milkmaids vending their wares, and scavenging pigs were among the common sights of the town. And there were gardens and trees in every part of it, and farms and byres among the densely packed surburban houses. Stow, its Elizabethan chronicler, used as a boy to fetch home from the nunnery farm in Goodman's field 'many a half-penny worth of milk, and never had less than three ale-pints for a half-penny in the summer, nor less than one ale-quart for a half-penny in the winter, always hot from the kine as the same was milked and strained.' And on May Day, he recalled, 'in the morning, every man, except impediment, would walk into the sweet meadows and green woods, there to rejoice their spirits with the beauty and savour of sweet flowers and with the harmony of birds.' After the stench and racket of the narrow streets and alleys they must have seemed sweet indeed. The Puritans, however, a fast-growing class even in Shakespeare's lifetime, took a far less kindly view of these outings; 'all the young men and maids, old men and wives,' one of them complained, 'run gadding overnight to the woods, groves, hills and mountains, where they spend all night in pleasant pastime' and, he added, in every sort of immorality.

If fields, farms, and woods—never more than a mile away to the north—were within the Londoner's easy reach, and the wooded heights of Hampstead and Highgate crowned his northern horizon, to the south lay the steep streets and alleys which sloped down to the river and its countless ships, boats, and wherries. Beyond it, except where the borough of Southwark crowded round the southern end of London Bridge, stretched marshes and green water-meadows, and beyond them the hanging woods of Penge and Norwood. The river was both London's southern boundary and principal highway and its link with the world, 'brimming with craft and commerce'.

No other city in Europe had a larger waterfront and none so famous a bridge. There was only one, but with its gabled houses and shops making a continuous street across it, its spired chapel, and gateway crowned with traitors' heads, its two cornmills and water works, its nineteen arches, with the rapids roaring under them, it was one of the wonders of the world.

Below the Bridge and guarding the Pool of London, where tall-masted ships unloaded and loaded before their ocean voyages, was the grim Norman Tower whose guns looked down on the swarming, unpoliced, libertarian city at its feet. Though no longer a place of royal residence, it served the purposes of a prison for State offenders, an armoury, a national mint, a public-record office, a menagerie, where some rather mangy lions and a few other beasts from Africa were kept for Londoners to gape at, and the treasury for the crown jewels. Stow described it as 'a citadel to defende or command the citie; a royall place for assemblies and treaties; a prison of Estate for the most dangerous offenders; the onely place of coynage for all England at this time; the armories for warlike provision; the Treasurie of the ornaments and jewels of the Crowne, and general conserver of the most recordes of the King's Courts of Justice at Westminster.' In his day, with its dungeons and torture-chambers, its block and tall scaffold on Tower Hill, its sentinel warders in their scarlet-and-gold royal liveries, it was still a very real reminder to the ambitious and great that the Crown would brook no rival.

The rough mob of the city loved the strong-nerved, sensible, and not-too-scrupulous Tudor sovereigns who kept the old feudal nobility in order, encouraged trade, and, respecting popular liberties, enforced peace. So did the lawyers in their gated and gardened Inns of Court and the country squires and yeomen in the shires who together made up the faithful, but by no means uncritical or subservient, Commons. The latter met periodically in the Parliament House at Westminster to vote reluctant supplies for the Queen or her indignant, bumbling Scottish successor, King James. Here they discussed business of State, and wrestled for their interests and beliefs with the royal Ministers and the hereditary nobles and lawn-sleeved prelates of the Church, assembled in Parliament's Upper House. By the time of the Stuart succession in 1603 the 'faithful Commons' were already a major power in the land and were soon to become a greater, and they were stoutly supported by the magistracy, populace, and rowdy apprentices of the City.

During Shakespeare's lifetime there were still a number of the great walled medieval palaces of the nobility—which figured so often in his historical plays—left in London, with their parks, gardens, and gatehouses. The traditional site for them was on the south side of the Strand—the highway which linked the City to royal Westminster. In summer their shady gardens, full of roses and fruit trees running down to the water's edge, and their owners' stately gilded and coloured barges moored before them, impressed the eye of travellers on the River.

The most splendid of all the buildings on the Thames belonged to the Crown. Five miles below London Bridge, among the Kentish meadows, was Greenwich where Queen Elizabeth had been born, where Shakespeare sometimes acted before her and her successor, King James, and from whose windows she had often watched her seamen setting forth on their exploring and trading voyages, 'her Majesty beholding the same with shaking her hand out of the window', as she did when Frobisher sailed past her riverside palace on his first voyage to find a north-west passage through the ice to the golden illusory East. Nearby, at Deptford, lay the famous ship in which Drake had circumnavigated the globe and on whose deck he had been knighted by his delighted sovereign. It became in the next age a popular resort for dinner and supper parties. Its natural decay was hastened by souvenir hunters who chipped so many pieces off its timbers that it gradually fell to pieces.

At the other end of London, a mile to the west of Temple Bar and close to Westminster Hall, St. Stephen's Chapel, where the Commons sat, and the Abbey—then without the towers which Wren was to add in the reign of Charles II—was the palace of Whitehall, the chief residence of the monarch and the seat of government. Here was a little city of its own, with walls, gates, chapels, halls, courtyards, lawns, and numerous apartments, and by the river an embankment planted with trees, and stairs for taking barge and boat. And here, begun a quarter of a century after Shakespeare's death, the Great Rebellion was to culminate in an English King stepping out of a window of his own Banqueting Hall to die at his subject's hands for having claimed that the royal prerogative could still override Parliament and the laws it made.

At no point did London stray far from the river. Except where the gardens of the greater houses were embanked, the houses came down to the waterside, where a succession of slippery stairs linked the city lanes to the life of the river. Here, as one approached the waterside, there started up from the wooden benches by the stairs a multitude of grizzly Tritons in sweaty shirts and short-backed doublets with badges on their arms, hallooing and hooting, 'Next oars!' and 'Eastward Ho!' and 'Westward Ho!' according to the direction in which they plied. The thousands of licensed watermen on the rolls of the City's Watermen's Company were ruled and licensed by the Lord

Mayor and his Water Bailiff, whose jurisdiction as Thames Conservator stretched from Staines bridge to the Medway. Their boats were of two kinds—sculls with one rower, and the faster 'oars' with two, in which one could travel with a favourable tide from the heart of London to Westminster in a quarter of an hour. Passengers sat on cushions and had a board to lean upon. But there was no covering except for a cloth spread over a few rough hoops in the stern, and, if a rainstorm came, one was usually soaked before there was time to raise it. The rich and great had barges with cabins, painted panels, and, by the middle of the seventeenth century, windows that slid up and down in sashes like those of coaches.

The great obstacle to travel on the river was London Bridge. Nervous passengers, frightened by the foam and roar of its cataracts, were wont to land at the Old Swan on the north bank and rejoin the boat 'below Bridge'. Save that one was apt to get 'soundly washed', shooting the rapids was not so bad as it looked; in flood-time one could take up fish with one's hand as they lay blinded by the thickness of the stream.

The language of the watermen was almost as great a wonder as the Bridge itself. It was a point of honour among them to exchange badinage of the coarsest kind with every passer-by; those acquainted with the adventures of Sir Roger de Coverly in the reign of the last Stuart will remember how this worthy gentleman, crossing to Vauxhall Gardens, was hailed as an 'old put' and asked if he was not ashamed to go a'wenching at his years. And this was mild abuse from a Thames waterman. Sometimes they met their match: a boatload of Lambeth gardeners, it was held, could return them as good as they gave and better. Knowing clients took a hand in the game themselves, and flung back gibes at the passing boats, almost as though this sort of thing were a requirement of river travel.

To those who took the foul language and rough humour of the watermen as part of the game, the river was full of delight. There were the gilded barges of the Sovereign and the great lords, and of the Lord Mayor and City Companies, with gorgeous liveried boatmen; the long, shallow lighters which carried malt and meat to feed London; the picturesque and very dirty vendors of fruit and strong waters, who with wheedling shouts brought their unlicensed skiffs alongside. When the weather was hot, one might pull off one's shoes and stockings and trail feet and fingers in the stream; at flood tide see the water coursing over the mill banks opposite Vauxhall and boats rowing in the streets of Westminster, or at low tide watch a daring boy wading through mud and pebbles from Whitehall to Lambeth. For the river served for pastime as well as business. Young Mr Pepys, born in London seventeen years after Shakespeare's death, would 'on a sudden motion' take up his wife and maids in a frolic and, with cold victuals and bottled ale, sail down to Gravesend to see the King's ships, or take the evening air as far as Greenwich or the Chelsea Neat House. At Barn Elms in his time ladies and courtiers came on June afternoons with bottles and baskets and chairs to sup under the trees by the waterside. And on moonlit nights the river took on a peculiar enchantment as parties of pleasure-seekers, in an age when the English were still a nation of music-makers, sang and accompanied themselves upon the water. Small wonder that the Londoner loved his river and went abroad on it whenever he could to look on 'the sun, the waters and the gardens of this fair city'.

Some time in the second decade of the seventeenth century—that great watershed of English history, when Shakespeare was living in retirement at Stratford-upon-Avon, when the first American settlers were struggling to secure their frail bridgehead in the transatlantic wilderness, when the child Milton was first feeling his way to beauty in the Bread Street house of his father, the music-loving Cheapside scrivener, and the men who were to make the Great Rebellion were growing up—Beaumont and Fletcher, in their comedy, *The Knight of the Burning Pestle*, put into the mouth of a simple London apprentice, summoning his fellows to their traditional May Day rites, the spirit, pride and sheer vigour of the late-Elizabethan and early Stuart capital.

London, to thee I do present the merry month of May;
Let each true subject be content to hear me what I say . . .
Rejoice, oh, English hearts, rejoice! Rejoice, oh, lovers
    dear!
Rejoice, oh, city, town, and country! Rejoice, eke every
    shire! . . .
With bells on legs, and napkins clean unto your shoulders
    tied,
With scarfs and garters as you please, and 'Hey for our
    town!' cried,
March out, and show your willing minds, by twenty and
    by twenty,
To Hogsdon or to Newington, where ale and cakes are
    plenty.
And let it ne'er be said for shame, that we the youths of
    London
Lay thrumming of our caps at home, and left our custom
    undone,
Up, then, I say, both young and old, both man and maid
    a-maying,

With drums, and guns that bounce aloud, and merry tabor
    playing!
Which to prolong, God save our King, and send his
    country peace,
And root out treason from the land! And so, my friends,
    I cease.

As one listens, one can see the colour and pageantry,
the crowded streets and bright garments, the painted,
gabled houses and spires and towers, the swift gravel
streams sparkling in the meadows on their way towards
Holborn and the Thames, and the concourse of
revelling Londoners setting out to the green-wood, as
their fathers had done before them and as their sons, in
a sadder and drabber age, were to do no longer.

6

Arrival in the Island

'For all that I have yet seen, give me old England.'
Edward Hyde, Earl of Clarendon

ONE USUALLY APPROACHED HER from the French
shore, travelling in the packet-boat from Calais. The
drawbacks were much as today, only they were more
acute, for not only was conversation in the boat apt to
be interrupted, as one disgusted traveller put it, by the
disorder which those who are not accustomed to the
sea are subject to, but such interruption was more
prolonged. Adverse winds might hold up the mail-boat
for several days, and it was fortunate if this delay
occurred in harbour rather than in mid-Channel. In
reasonably fair weather the crossing took seven hours.

Even before landing the sensitive traveller was made
aware of the island, for, if the wind blew from off her
cliffs, scents of thyme and sheep on the uplands were
borne out to sea. Other scents, too, for the little town
of Dover was as innocent of the art of sanitation as any
in Europe. Nestling beneath her castle, she presented
an inviting appearance, which closer acquaintance
modified. Both castle and harbour works were much
decayed, and the shingle was constantly drifted by
storms into the fairway, so that on more than one

occasion the Mayor was forced to summons reluctant householders with shovels to the beach for the customary labour of clearing the harbour. And once, in 1662, a government office in London was aroused from lethargy by the arrival from the storm-beleaguered town of a missive fearfully endorsed: 'In haste, post haste, or all's lost; port, town and people.'

Landing was attended by formalities—by the officers of the Customs with prying eyes, by those of the Castle on watch for undesirable entrants (a constant succession of whom were lodged in its dungeons and who, aided by bribery, almost as constantly escaped), and, in the case of very distinguished visitors, by the Deputy Master of Ceremonies sent down from London to do the honours.

For more ordinary mortals welcome was accorded by the younger and lazier inhabitants of the town, who, leaving their games or their loafing, accompanied them to their inns with such affronts as they deemed appropriate to the species of foreigner before them. Of these the most common was the cry of 'A Monsieur, a Monsieur', accompanied by a certain mocking and dandified gait; it was best to accept this with a smile, for opposition to the island proletariat quickly brought out its more quarrelsome traits, and jeers would then give way to angry growls of 'French dogs' and threats of worse.

Not that they were unreasonable. Those of the more educated class were not averse to criticism; in fact, as they sat around the newcomer over the inn fire they invited him to express his views on their customs and character, and even seemed to take pleasure in hearing the truth; only if it were adverse they showed plainly by their laughter that they did not believe it. They appeared to have plenty of leisure and to be in no particular hurry about anything, spending much of their time drinking, taking tobacco, and talking, disapprovingly for the most part, about the Government; nor, for all this apparent laziness—and even the poorest were slothful—did they seem to suffer the flagrant destitution so noticeable in a continental town. And when, after the night's stay, they presented the bill, it was obvious that they were accustomed to gentlemen with well-lined purses.

From Dover the traveller climbed the hill and rode over the downs—'a pleasant champain country with the sea and the coast of France clear in view'—to Canterbury. There was a wide choice of transport. Those in a hurry might gallop the twelve miles in an hour's time on the excellent post-horses with which the island abounded, for the English, though lazy in the ordinary concerns of life, were rapid in travelling; the very country people rode to market 'as it were for a benefice.' Or, if one shirked the heavy post-horse charge of 3d. a mile (with an extra 4d. for the guide at each stage), and did not mind being made a little sick, one could travel more slowly in a wagon drawn by six horses and directed by a gentleman with a whip who walked beside carrying on a perpetual interchange of personalities with his passengers.

The sights of the road revealed England. Gentlemen's coaches, with six horses drawing them and much colour and gilt of emblazonry, travellers, carriers, and drovers passing and repassing, country-folk going to market, and, in the fields or on the open downs beside the grass highway, haymakers and shepherds at their business. Occasionally there would be some special excitement: a royal courier riding post, or, if it were assize time, the splendid inconvenience of being jostled out of a narrow lane by the coaches and horses of the judges and lawyers pressing forward to the next circuit town.

Beyond the road the landscape stretched into blue horizons. 'The country and the grass here', wrote one who saw them for the first time in 1670, 'seemed to me to be finer and of a better colour than in other places.' Trees were everywhere, stirred to life by sea-breezes that blew perpetually across the island, carrying with them clouds which gave changing lights and shades to every contour. And in the Weald beyond the downs there were orchards of apple and cherry, so many that from an eminence it looked as though the whole land was given over to forest. Here, too—and this was unlike the greater part of the country, which was still open—there were enclosures with quickset hedges surrounding the meadows; parks, too, with smooth parterres and bowling-greens before houses which, though inferior in grandeur to the châteaux of France, had with their homely timbering and long peaked roofs a trim and intimate dignity of their own. The general effect was that of a planted garden.

Of the weather one was made conscious from the first; for it was much as it is today. All that could be predicted of it for certain was that it would never be the same for long. Summers of rare loveliness, when the fruit and corn ripened to a bumper harvest and July flowers were out in May, and Christmases bright with snow and holly, lived as now in the consecrated memory of old men; more usually the climate showered down its variegated blessings with humorous inappropriateness. 'A verie tempestious slabby day' would be succeeded by a night of 'brave moonshine'; 'a good misling morning' by an afternoon gale; and a hard frost by 'a monstrous great thaw' that sent everyone unexpectedly skidding down the streets. One January it was so fine that dusty roads were haunted by flies and the rose-bushes were full of leaves—'glorious and warm, even to amazement, for this time of year'; in the same May, after two months of almost continuous rain, the bishops declared a fast; only when the time came the weather had changed to drought, so that they were forced to compromise according to Anglican wont by keeping the day half as a fast and half as a feast. Yet foreigners, though they hated the white fogs which haunted the country ditches and crept even into the towns, praised the general salubrity of the climate: there was pure air, plenty of wind, and an absence of anything that enervated. And the soft moisture of the atmosphere gave the land ever-changing beauty and colour—the blues and greys and silver whites which enchanted every horizon.

Canterbury was the first town reached. At a distance, its cathedral rose majestic above the surrounding walls; nearer at hand it was seen, like the town itself, to be in that decay which, since the days of the Reformation, had befallen the cathedral cities of England, and which the deliberate desecrations of the Commonwealth men in recent years had only intensified. Still the general air of ruin was qualified, as in all things English, by a certain pleasant and intimate charm. There were ancient prebendal houses of crumbling stone set in gardens of blossom and fresh green, and in the narrow streets of the city itself the houses, so low that occupants of middle height were forced to stoop perpetually, nestled together till their eaves almost touched. To a foreigner it seemed remarkable that all the windows were glazed and mostly without shutters; those of the lower rooms had curtains and iron bars for privacy and safety, and those of the upper casements which opened in the middle, throwing at night a delightful air of candle-lit intimacy on to the street below. Another peculiarity was the bay windows, which, set in little angles and projections of the houses, enabled a householder to overlook the street in both directions without being himself observed. And behind each house, which was thus in itself a small castle, were gardens and meadows; for *rus in urbe* was the English rule.

Leaving Canterbury on the Feversham road, the traveller entered a land of apples, hops, and cherries. High two-wheeled carts drawn by oxen, bearing hops for the local maltsters or Kentish pippins and russets for the Medway and Three Cranes Wharf, herds of red bullocks with crumpled horns from the Weald pastures, and troops of labourers with scythe and sickle tramping for refreshment to the next village, showed the agricultural interests of the neighbourhood. Indeed, Kent was a kind of agriculturist's Mecca, with its great hop gardens, it orchards of cherries, pears, and apples, its tidy habits of cultivation, and its high wages. Its only drawback for the labourer, who in harvest-time could earn as much as 2s. a day (almost double what he could hope for elsewhere), were its notorious agues. But of these the traveller was as yet unaware.

Feversham, a long, straggling town, encompassed the road for over a mile. Beyond the town, coast and road ran for a time within sight of each other, until from the higher ground west of Sittingbourne the traveller caught the gleam of the Medway. A few miles later he entered the twin towns of Chatham and

Rochester. Here were the King's naval arsenals, with lanes of storehouses going down to the water's edge, and a main street which stretched for half a league along the Medway until it crossed it by a stone bridge, adorned by a parapet of iron balusters set there by the authorities to catch suicides and hats.

After Rochester the way divided. Here experienced travellers left the main London high road through Dartford, and bore riverwards to Gravesend. In doing so they were wise to seek each other's company, for the road passed over Gad's Hill, notorious since the days of Falstaff for its robberies. Here on a summer's dawn in 1676 a highwayman on a bay mare robbed a gentleman as he came over the brow of the hill; then, setting spurs to his horse, crossed the ferry to Tilbury (where the delays attendant on tide and a leisurely waterman kept him champing for nearly an hour) and hastened through the Essex lanes to Chelmsford and thence over the downs to Cambridge and Huntingdon, where he rested his horse. An hour later he was mounted again and, galloping up the Great North Road, miraculously reached York the same afternoon, where, after changing his clothes, he repaired to the bowling-green and, singling out the Lord Mayor, made a small wager with him on the fortunes of the game, being careful to ask the time as he did so. All which subsequently proved an irrefutable alibi, and not only earned the highwayman, whose name was Nicks, a triumphant acquittal, but a private interview with His Sacred Majesty King Charles II, who was entranced by the whole story and endowed his prudent subject with the sobriquet of 'Swift Nicks'.

At Gravesend, a little snug town of watermen's houses, one took the ferry for London. Here outgoing ships were forced to anchor for a last visit from the Customs officials, and there was always a fleet of vessels riding in the road. With the tide in one's favour, one could reach London in four hours, either by wherry or, if one chose to be less exclusive and more economical, by the common tilt boat which carried up to sixty passengers at 8*d*. a head. One had one's money's worth, not only in the passage, but in the sights—fleets of colliers beating up the river with Newcastle coal, Barking smacks with mackerel, sailing under such clouds of canvas that it seemed they must at any moment upset, hoys from Deal and Sandwich bringing the produce of Kent to London, and merchantmen bound for the Indies or Mediterranean. As one proceeded, the chalk-pits and marshes near Gravesend gave way to almost continuous villages and yards busy with ships' carpenters making vessels to take possession of the watery realms which the Navigation Acts were giving England. For those who loved the sight of busy mankind it was the most beautiful river in Europe.

At Woolwich travellers crowded to the port gunwale for a statelier sight, where in the deep water against the shore the King's gilded yachts lay against the wall of the dockyard. A mile beyond, under the trees of its sloping park lay royal Greenwich, with its old, rambling palaces, sadly plundered in the late troubles, lying in ruins, and on the lawns that stretched before the Queen's House, which Inigo Jones had built under the hill, a new palace of white stone rising by the waterside. Then, in a moment, one was in the grey, windswept waters of Long Reach, with one unbroken arsenal stretching along either shore—the greatest shipbuilding centre in the world, save, perhaps, the yards at

Schiedam by Amsterdam. Yet within living memory what was a continuous street of buildings along the water had been a lonely tract of marsh, broken only by the gallows on which condemned pirates had been wont to hang till three tides had covered them. And so, at the bend by Limehouse one came to London. Before lay the Tower, the many-arched house-crowned bridge, and the Thames flowing out to meet the sea between a hundred spires and a hundred thousand roofs.

7

Pepys and the Great Fire

'And Paul's is burned and all Cheapside.'

Pepys's Diary, 4 September 1666

ON THE FIRST DAY OF SEPTEMBER 1666, a Saturday, Pepys with his wife, her paid companion, Mercer, and his colleague Sir William Penn, took the afternoon off from the Office and went to the playhouse. There they were horribly frightened to see young Killigrew and some of the wild young sparks from Court, but, by concealing themselves, escaped detection. Then, after a merry jaunt to the cakes and meadows of Islington, the Clerk of the Acts of the Royal Navy returned home, his mind dwelling much on the thought of gilding the backs of his books in the carved and glazed presses which Sympson, the joiner, had made for them that summer. His new closet, he reflected, had been set mighty clean against the morrow, when he was entertaining guests to view it for the first time, and all his worldly affairs prospered. The wind was blowing strongly from the east, after long drought.

About three o'clock on Sunday morning Pepys was called from his bed by his maids, who had sat up late setting things ready against the day's feast, with news of a fire in the City. With his unfailing curiosity, he slipped on his nightgown and went to the window to look; he judged it to be at the backside of Mark Lane and, after watching for a little while, went back to bed.

He was up again by seven, and when he looked out the fire seemed to be further off than it was and smaller. So he went to his closet to see that everything was ready for his party. Here the little maid Jane Birch (now returned to the household) came to him to tell him that they were saying that over three hundred houses had been burnt in the night and that the fire was now raging along the steep slope of Fish Street above the Bridge.

He made himself ready and went out, walking up to the Tower, where he got Sir John Robinson's little son to take him up one of the turrets whence he could see what was taking place. Half a mile to the west lay London Bridge with its northern houses all in flames and a great fire blazing between Thames Street and the river, where a huddled infinity of timber-built, pitch-coated little houses and warehouses of oil, tallow, and spirits provided fuel enough in that dry, windy weather to light all London. His heart misgave him at the sight and was full of trouble for little Betty Howlett—now married to young Michell, the bookseller's son, and living near the 'Old Swan' in the very heart of those flames—and for his old sweetheart Sarah who dwelt upon the Bridge; his loves were being burnt out like wasps.

He went down and spoke to the Lieutenant of the Tower, who confirmed his worst fears: then took boat and went up through the Bridge, seeing as he passed through the steep piers the houses of his friends blazing beside the water. As he watched, unconsciously the great artist that was within him took possession of his being; and for an hour he remained as an eye-witness for posterity storing up all he saw—the scorching, untamable, giant flames, the householders crazy to remove their goods, flinging them into lighters alongside or into the very river itself, the 'poor people staying in their houses as long as till the very fire touched them and then running into boats or clambering from one pair of stairs by the waterside to another.' Even the pigeons, the watching eyes of the diarist beheld, were loath to leave their houses but hovered about the windows and balconies till their wings were singed and they fell down. The flaming shadow of death, roaring like a giant, was driving the love of home and property from their age-long habitations before his very eyes.

But when he saw that no one in that universal desire of each man to save his own was making any attempt to stay the fire, which the wind was driving into the heart of the City, the administrator took command of the artist, and he bade the boatman row him swiftly to Whitehall. Here he found them all at chapel, but, giving his tidings, he was brought to the King and the Duke of York, to whom he told what he had seen, saying that unless his Majesty gave orders that houses should be pulled down nothing could stop the fire. They seemed much troubled and commanded him to go to the Lord Mayor and bid him destroy all in the path of the flames. With this errand he drove to St. Paul's and then walked through the narrow panic-stricken lanes till he found that unhappy magistrate, with a handkerchief about his neck, crying like a fainting woman: 'Lord! what can I do? I am spent; people will not obey me. I have been pulling down houses, but the fire overtakes us faster than we can do it.' And then walked on. His useless errand accomplished, Pepys also walked on. Once more as he did so the artist came out, seeing the flying distracted crowds and the churches filling with goods borne there by people who at this time, had things been otherwise, he reflected, should have been quietly praying within. Then, it being midday, he went home to entertain his guests. But his dinner party was not a success, for the hearts of those who sat down were elsewhere and Pepys's intention that they should please themselves with the sight of his fine new closet was not fulfilled. And as soon as they could, they went away.

Once more Pepys went out into the streets—'full of nothing but people and horses and carts loaden with goods, ready to run over one another, and removing goods from one burned house to another.' He saw familiar friends passing through that troubled kaleidoscope of driven humanity, the King and the Duke of York in their barge going down the river to take command of their capital, the Thames crowded with goods of all sorts—'and there was hardly', he noted for the instruction of posterity, 'one lighter or boat in three . . . but there was a pair of virginalls in it.' Then, as it grew dark, the air filled with flakes of fire, and he and his wife, Elizabeth, unable to endure the scorching heat any longer, crossed the river to a little alehouse on Bankside and there watched that terrible spectacle. As night deepened, the fire seemed to grow 'more and more, and in corners and upon steeples, and between churches and houses, as far as we could see up the hill of the City, in a most horrid, malicious bloody flame, not like the fine flame of an ordinary fire . . . We staid', he wrote, 'till, it being darkish, we saw the fire as only one entire arch of fire from this to the other side of the bridge, and in a bow up the hill for an arch of above a mile long; it made me weep to see it. The churches, houses and all on fire and flaming at once; and a horrid noise the flames made and the cracking of houses at their ruin.'

When at last they went home, with a bright moon in the sky and fire all over the earth, they found poor Tom Hayter, who was always in trouble, come with a few of his goods which he had saved from his house in Fish Street Hill to take shelter with his master. Pepys gladly offered him a bed and received his goods, but with the fire creeping north and east as well as driving west-wards with the wind, he felt that it was time to move his own; the yard was already full of his colleague Sir William Batten's carts, come up from Waltham-stow. So all night long the household tramped up and down the wooden stairs, carrying money in iron chests into the cellar, and bags of gold and boxes of paper into the garden. Hayter trying to sleep in the troubled house, the carts rumbling into the yard from the country, the smell and crackling of fire and the moon looking down serene on the bewildered doings of men, made up the sum of this night. Before it ended, the fire was raging from Queenhithe in the west to Cannon Street on the north, and eastwards beyond the lower end of Botolph Lane.

At about four o'clock on Monday morning, Samuel Pepys, Clerk of the Acts, riding in a cart of Batten's, packed high with his goods and arrayed only in his nightgown, set out for Bethnal Green. Here at Sir William Rider's, already crowded with the belongings of his friends, he left his most treasured possessions (among them the volumes of his Diary). Then through the crowd of flying people and carts, he fought his way back to the burning City. All that Monday, a glorious summer's day, he and his poor wife, weary and dazed for lack of sleep, packed up their household goods and, bearing them over Tower Hill, loaded them into a lighter at the quay above Tower Dock. Meanwhile the fire burned ever more fiercely, spreading northwards to devour all Lombard Street, the Poultry, and Cornhill, and tumbling the Royal Exchange and forty churches in that universal ruin. Beside the river it ran westwards a further half-mile to Baynard's Castle, but its easterly advance was restricted by the wind. Yet even here it crept along Eastcheap and Thames Street, a couple of hundred yards nearer Seething Lane.

In the midst of all this horror Mrs Pepys, like a woman inspired, contrived to give Mercer notice. That young lady (whose breasts, though she knew it not, her husband had of late taken to fondling as she dressed him of a morning),* had without leave, but very naturally, gone to help her mother move her things. Elizabeth, tracking her down, had upbraided her furiously, at which Mrs Mercer had shouted back that her daughter was no prentice girl to ask leave every time she went abroad. The angry housewives in battle, while the great fire pursued its course less than a quarter of a mile away, was the last scene in Mercer's sojourn. She departed that night, while her erstwhile master and mistress lay down in turn to snatch a few hours' sleep on a little quilt of Will Hewer's in the Office.

Tuesday the 4th, was the greatest day of the fire. Ranged now far to the north, its flaming battalions poured westwards in irresistible strength over the doomed City. Early in the morning it reached St.

---

* '. . . they being the finest that ever I saw in my life, that is the truth of it.' *Diary*, 19 June 1666.

Paul's, and, while the leaden roof poured in streams of burning lava into the nave below, flames leapt rejoicing across the valley of the Fleet on to the wooden houses of Salisbury Court and St. Bride's, all but encircling the Duke of York and his soldiers—who were gallantly blowing up houses on Ludgate Hill—in an inescapable ring of fire. Eastwards the foe came up both sides of narrow Thames Street with infinite fury, while Batten and Pepys dug a deep pit in the Navy Office garden in which to lay, the one his wine and the other his papers and Parmesan cheese. Threatened with the immediate destruction of his home, Pepys that afternoon received sudden inspiration—to send for the naval dockyard hands from Woolwich and Deptford to pull down houses and save the Office. He communicated these thoughts to Sir William Penn, who was sitting melancholy by his side in the garden. The latter at once went down the river to summon this help, while Pepys (even at this juncture methodically taking a copy) wrote to Coventry for the Duke's permission to pull down houses, there being an ancient rule of the City that whoever destroyed his neighbour's dwelling should be at the expense of rebuilding it.

That night the fire was in Fenchurch Street to the north of the lane and had already reached the 'Dolphin' in Tower Street. Pepys and his wife sat down to a last sad supper in their house with Mr Turner, the Petty Purveyor, and his wife as their guests. Somehow they contrived to be a little merry. Only when they looked out, the horrid glamour of the sky, 'all in a fire in the night', terrified them almost out of their wits; it looked as though the whole heaven was in flames. Throughout the night, the sound of explosions kept them from sleeping: the authorities, bent on saving the powder store in the Tower, were now blowing up houses all along Tower Street. At two in the morning, after again lying a brief while on Hewer's quilt in the Office, Pepys was called up with news that the fire was at the bottom of Seething Lane. There being now no hope, he took his wife, Will Hewer and Jane, with £2,350 in gold, by boat to Woolwich. Then leaving them at Mr Sheldon's in the Yard (after charging his wife and Will never to leave the room in which the gold was lodged without one of them to keep watch on it) he returned to London to survey the ruins of his home.

But when he got back at seven in the morning his house and the Navy Office were still standing. The men from the Yards, whom Penn had brought up in the night, had done their business; and at Barking Church, its porch and dial already burnt, the fire had been for the moment at least stopped, though from the north flames still threatened. Then, the artist overcoming even the man of property, Pepys climbed to the top of the rescued steeple and surveyed the scene—'the saddest sight of desolation that ever I saw, everywhere great fires, oil cellars and brimstone . . . burning . . . the fire being spread as far as I could see it.'

Then, having good hopes that the worst was over—for everywhere the King and the Duke of York with their soldiers and volunteers had been opposing its course with rope and powder—he dined on cold meat at Sir William Penn's, the first proper meal he had eaten in three days, and walked abroad to see the town. Over the smouldering ruins he made his way, as his fellow-diarist, Evelyn, did two days later, clambering over piles of smoking rubbish, the ground so hot beneath his feet that it scorched the soles of his shoes. Fenchurch, Gracechurch, and Lombard Streets were all dust, the Exchange a blackened skeleton, and Moorfields full of poor wretches sitting among their goods. He noted Anthony Joyce's house still burning, the buckled glass that had fallen from the windows of the Mercers' Chapel, and the poor cat, its hair all burned off its body, which he saw being taken out of a hole in a chimney. So he went home, and, as the air was still full of flying sparks, and rumours were abroad of Dutch and French spies carrying fireballs to spread the flames, he set the dockyard men to guard the Office all night, giving them beer and bread and cheese. Then he fell asleep, all sense of time lost.

But that wonderful curiosity did not allow him to sleep long, and he was up before five. At the gate of the Office as he went out, he met Gauden, the Victualler, hurrying to beg the aid of his men to fight a new fire that had broken out at Bishopsgate. So Pepys went along with his dockyard men and helped to put it out, which they did in a little while; it was strange, he reflected, to see how hard the women worked fetching water and how they would then scold for a drink and be as drunk as devils. Then, his work done, and being all in dirt from head to foot, Dapper Dicky, as his friends called him, took boat to Westminster to buy a shirt and some gloves and get himself trimmed. And as he went up the river he saw the sad sight of the ruined shores, with no house standing from Tower Bank to the Temple. Of the old City within the wall, scarcely a sixth part remained; thirteen thousand houses had been burnt, leaving a hundred thousand people homeless.

Such was the strange and terrible interlude which broke the course of Pepys's life. He for his part had been wonderfully fortunate—'the Lord of Heaven make me thankful and continue me therein!' His goods, scattered at Woolwich, Deptford, and Bethnal Green, were all safe, and when, a week later, the dockyard labourers had ceased to tramp all night through the Office and his house was made clean, he brought them all home by cart and barge (all save two little sea-pictures which were somehow mislaid) and to his infinite joy lay with his wife in his chamber again. Only, he added, 'I do lack Mercer or somebody in the house to sing with.' But though he tried to entice her back, the lady would not return.

For though Pepys might resume the even tenor of his ways—though he might go abroad in fine clothes again* or in a single afternoon (less than a week after the fire ceased) enjoy both Martin's wife and Bagwell's—the background of his life was changed for ever. Around the Navy Office still stood the familiar houses, and at Westminster and at Whitehall there were trees and green grass and the wonted dwellings of men. But between the two lay a vast wilderness of horror. Walking or riding from Whitehall one approached it, as one visitor to London recalled, passing the untouched palaces of the nobility which still lined the south side of the Strand. But once through Temple Bar, a double line of houses ended two hundred yards away in a desolation of blackened rubble and white ashes, stretching as far as the eye could see and broken only by the ruin of old St. Paul's and the tottering towers of churches. Here for many months the stench of smoke of subterranean fires assailed the traveller. Nor was it safe at night to pass by for fear of the lawless and homeless men who lurked among the shadows; half a year later when his Majesty's Clerk of the Acts had

---

* 'Up betimes and shaved myself after a week's growth, but Lord! how ugly I was yesterday, and how fine today!' *Diary*, 17 September 1666.

occasion to pass through the ruins, he sat in the coach with his sword drawn.

But being English, Pepys dwelt as little as possible on all this. From shades and horrors he turned to the normal and familiar; recorded cheerfully, even before the fire was fully burnt out, how house property in his part of the town was soaring in value, how the citizens congregated at the still-standing Gresham College to gossip and bargain, and what speedy plans were being made for rebuilding the City. Of that mysterious country, whose horrid landscape he had seen for a brief while, he did not speak; only in dreams, lying (when the memory of it was still fresh) in Penn's naked bed with nothing but his drawers on, or long after beside Elizabeth in his own familiar room, did he revisit it with the fear of fire in his heart.

8

Coaching up the North Road

IMAGE YOURSELF about to take a journey from a little town somewhere in the northern midlands to London, not today but three hundred years ago. It is a town in a remote, hilly district, a day's journey from the great main road which links London to the north and where the new-fashioned stage-coaches run. Like most of your neighbours and indeed most Englishmen of the time, you have never been to London or anywhere farther than a day's ride to the nearest Assize town, where you once went when you had a small law-suit about a field. But this is to be a much greater journey on very important business—nothing else could justify the time and expense of such an undertaking—and you have been putting it off all the winter till the rains stopped and the floods subsided and the roads dried a little after their annual drenching.

Of course, though you are going on business, it is all rather an adventure. You have never done such a journey before and in the course of your life you are never likely to again. So though you rather dread the dangers and discomforts, you are rather thrilled. For a long time past you have been making preparations, buying clothes for the journey, and discussing with your neighbours the best way of reaching London.

After thinking it over you have decided to ride to the nearest posting-town on the Great North Road, where you have booked a place in one of the new-fashioned flying-coaches that ply from York to London during the summer in the almost incredibly short space of four days—that is, as the advertisement in the town coffee-house is careful to point out, 'if God permit'. There are only three coaches a week, so you were careful to book your seat a month or so before, and have paid 35s. for it with an extra 10s. premium for the advance booking. It seems a lot of money, when you remember that that sum is equivalent to at least nine or ten times as much as it would be today, but, short of being a gentleman with a private coach of your own or a Croesus who can afford to hire a post-chaise, it is the most comfortable and rapid means of travel available— and, as you are never likely to have the chance of doing the journey again, it seems well worth it.

Well, the great day arrives. Very early, before it is light—for with the vast distances you have to cover, every hour of daylight is precious—you get up and dress by candlelight in the travelling clothes you have bought or borrowed for the occasion—high boots thickly beeswaxed, a thick leather riding-suit and a long cloak coming down to your spurs to keep off the dust and mud. And, knowing there may be footpads or highwaymen, you are careful to add a pair of pistols and a sword—the one your father wore at the battle of Edgehill. Then, clanking a little ponderously over the cobble-stones and waking up some of your neighbours as you go, you make your way down the dark familiar streets to the George Inn, where for the sum of 3d. a mile for the sixty miles or so you have to cover you have hired a horse from your friend, the host, who being also the local postmaster aways keeps three or four post-horses for travellers. The ostler is waiting with it in the courtyard beside the mounting-stone, so you hastily swallow your morning draught of mulled ale and pull yourself into the saddle. A guide from the inn, who is to accompany you as far as the coaching town, is waiting also with a led horse on which your luggage is slung.

A minute later you are trotting over the cobble-stones and out into the country with the guide and the led horse beside you. In front, winding over hill and dale, stretches your road. It is not a smooth white metalled road with clearly defined sides like a modern road, but a soft grassy trackway, marked by horse hoofs and ruts. Near the town the ruts have been ploughed up by the parish road-plough which is taken from its home under the church porch every spring for this purpose. But soon these signs of civilisation vanish, and the winter's ruts, often five or six feet deep, are untouched, with only an occasional sprinkling of stones or faggots thrown loosely down in the worst places. You soon slacken pace and subside into a walk. In the muddier parts you find it better to leave the highway and ride beside it in the fields. The road seems to have gone native: sometimes a broad grassy trackway with the hedges and bushes cut back twenty yards or more on either side, as the regulations against robbers require, and at others only a narrow lane between high hedges and so narrow in places that you have to ride in single file to avoid being scratched by the brambles. Presently it becomes hilly and the track full of large smooth pebbles which make the horses slip, so that you are forced every now and then to dismount and lead them. And at the bottom of every valley there

is a stream and a ford through which you splash. There
are no bridges in this district, except for a few quaking,
shaking structures of neglected stone or wood, full of
holes and so narrow that you can scarcely persuade
your horse to cross. It is a lonely part of the world, and
you meet few people on the road. They are mostly
farmers and peasants going about their business. Their
produce, you notice, is carried on wooden frames
loaded high and corded on the horses' backs instead
of being slung on either side in the usual panniers.
This is because of the narrowness of the lanes, your
guide tells you.

On the crest of the hills you can see the country
spread before you—far wilder than the England of
today—a rolling plain with few hedges or fences, and
here and there dark with great woods and forests.
Much of it is waste and heath: only round the villages,
where you stop for a few minutes for refreshment at a
smoking alehouse hung with spiders' webs, are there
ploughed fields, and these without hedges and cut up
into innumerable strips like vast allotments. Between
the villages there is little sign of cultivation, save for a
few scraggy cattle and tiny sheep, and occasionally
some geese and swine, with here and there a wretched
hovel of sticks and straw where the smoke of some
poor squatters rises into the early summer air.

So you ride all day, till your seat grows sore beneath
you and you begin to wish you had spent a few more
days in the winter accustoming yourself to horseback.
Your boots are splashed high with mud and your cloak
and saddle-cloth thick with dust. Once you lose your
way, for there are so many tracks branching our to left
and right that even the guide is often puzzled.
Fortunately a friendly pedlar, sleeping by the roadside

after selling his wares at some lonely hill hamlet, sets you on your way again. Only once do you see a signpost—the very first in these parts, your companion tells you—and your best guides are the church spires and belfries of the villages along the way. Once, as you reach the top of a hill, there is a more ominous landmark: a tall gibbet and on it, creaking and swaying in the wind, a fading corpse with a few poor shreds of clothing hanging from it and a cluster of ugly kites hovering overhead. The guide tells you, with a grim laugh, that the corpse was once a highwayman, who has been hung to discourage others on the spot where once he committed his robberies.

A little before it begins to get dark you descend a long winding hill and start to cross a great plain. Presently the road turns into a narrow causeway, paved with rough stones, and on either side a dark marsh from which an evil-smelling white mist is beginning to rise and the sound of strange birds calling out eerily! It reminds you of the narrow road across the Valley of the Shadow of Death of which you have been reading in Mr Bunyan's, the nonconformist preacher's book, the *Pilgrim's Progress*. Suddenly there is the sound of a jingling bell, and then eyes shine before you in the gathering darkness and shadowy forms loom up on the causeway. A man calls out angrily, and you feel for your pistols. But a moment later you are reassured, for it is only a train of pack-horses carrying ironware towards the town from which you have come. Still, it is inconvenient enough for, being only two to their fifty, you and your guide have to clamber down the slippery side of the causeway into the mud below while the long procession of laden horses winds by like an infinitely slow luggage-train, the warning bell jingling on the leading horse and the pack-horse men swearing and cursing out of the darkness.

Wearily, and muddy now up to the saddle-girths, you lead your horse back on to the causeway and remount. Soon it is quite dark. You are hungry and cold and fear that the fenny mist around you will breed an ague, and ache in every limb of your body. Then, far away, you hear the sound of church bells and see faint lights, and the guide tells you that your journey is almost done. It is past eight o'clock and you have been in the saddle with a few brief halts since five in the morning. But you have ridden the fifty miles you had to travel—in winter you could not have done half the distance—and here before you is the posting town on the Great North Road. A few minutes later your horse, pricking up his ears, canters into the courtyard of the chief inn of the place—the station from which the London coach starts in the morning. It has already arrived and disgorged its passengers, and you can see its great shadowy form in the darkness.

A servant comes running out with a lantern, an ostler takes your horse, and a moment later you are being escorted up a broad oak staircase to a room where, since you are resolved to spare no expense and have the best of everything, a fire is quickly lit and a cup of sack brought you by mine host himself. With a bow he asks you whether you will have your supper served in your chamber or dine with your fellow-travellers of the morrow in the ordinary downstairs. You elect the latter. After a servant has pulled off your great boots and taken off your heavy cloak and sword, you go downstairs and join the company in a smoke-filled room before a mighty fire. Here you eat heartily, drink deep of the inn-keeper's incomparable strong waters, and fall asleep to an accompaniment of mine host's broad jokes and long stories about jackasses and horse-races. At last you stagger up to bed and are soon snoring loudly, unwoken even by the fleas and the croaking of the frogs under the floor, which are the hostlery's only defect—for it is a capital house and one of England's most famous inns.

You are aroused early in the morning—just before it is light—and to music. For there in the narrow street below your window is the town band come to give you and your fellow travellers a *levite*—a favour for which, though unasked, you have to vail or tip them, as you also have the ostler, the servants, and your guide of yesterday. Then you swallow your morning draft—a bottle of Northdown ale and some pickled oysters—and proceed to take your place in the coach. It is a formidable-looking vehicle with a domed roof and a square body covered with black leather and studded with brass nails, and swung on leather straps suspended from tall axle-trees. In front sits the coachman with a vast red cloak and wide laced sleeves, and in front of him six great black shire horses pawing the stones impatiently. The luggage is strapped on to a platform on the back, and, after a scramble for the best seat in which you are a little too slow for your more experienced fellow-travellers, you take your seat, a gentleman of leisure, in the boot of the coach.

It is a fine day, so you and your five fellow-passengers open the leather flap that serves for window and look out at the sights of the road. They are worth seeing, for this is the greatest road in the country, and half England seems afoot or a-horse. The road is much broader than the one you travelled yesterday, though still only a soft, ill-defined trackway of grass and trampled earth, for the raised and metalled road which ran here vanished centuries ago. All over it horsemen and pedestrians, herds of cattle and livestock and country carts drawn by oxen and horses are winding and zigzagging to avoid the holes and the enormous ruts into which it has been cut by the winter traffic. The coach creaks, sways, rolls, and plunges—it is travelling at a smart pace of five miles an hour, unthinkable till a few years back for wheeled traffic—and a young gentleman in the corner complains that he feels sick and wishes that he had taken the advice of his father, the Yorkshire squire, and ridden to London in the good old-fashioned way. Still, it is something to feel that you are travelling in one of the fastest vehicles on one of the fastest roads in the world: there is a good deal to be said for progress after all. It is better than crawling along in a stage-wagon, with thirty other passengers of all classes crowded together on the wooden floor under the arched cloth hood and covering a bare twelve or fifteen miles a day: it would take a fortnight to reach London that way. Just at that moment you start to pass one—a vast, long covered wagon with eight horses one behind the other, with plumes and bells, and the wagoner with a long whip walking beside. He and the guard of your coach exchange such a volley of broad country oaths and jests that the lady opposite you blushes crimson.

The sights of the road are never-ending; country carts and laden farm horses, pedlars and chapmen with their packs and trays, pedestrians with bundles on their backs and red-faced Justices with their grinning servants riding to their business; a travelling merchant with three or four led horses carrying samples of cloth, and every now and then a gentlewoman riding pillion behind husband or groom. Once or twice in the hour you pass a gentleman's coach, emblazoned with heraldry, the six fine horses drawing it shaking their brightly coloured reins and a footman in livery going before to open the gates and remove boulders and other obstacles from the road. About midday, just before you draw up at the inn of a tiny market town to dine, you see a royal courier riding post with His Majesty's arms and mails. All the while the country-folk are passing and repassing, going to market or driving their flocks, while in the great fields beside the open road haymakers and shepherds are attending to their business.

Every few miles the coach splashes through the ford of some stream, while tiny runlets and water-courses cross the road almost constantly. Once there is a halt of several minutes while the coach waits its turn at a narrow stone bridge over a broad river. All this, though the sun is shining brightly, keeps the coach well plastered with mud, and at least twice you are forced to alight while a score or so of country labourers shoulder it out of a deep rut into which it has fallen and almost overturned. It is obvious that all this wheeled traffic, which has recently superseded the purely foot- and horse-travelling of earlier days, is playing havoc with the English road system: it is no longer any use doing, as the old statute that governed highway maintenance laid down, leaving the roads alone that they may 'grow better of themselves'. With so many wheels, wind and sun are not enough, and even the new Acts of Parliament, which restrict the number of draught-horses and insist on a regulation thickness of wheel-rims, seems to do little good. Frequently in the neighbourhood of villages you pass gangs of labourers, cutting away overgrowing brambles from the sides of the highway and shovelling loose earth into the worst holes. But they work lazily enough, for the law, which enforces on each parishioner six days a year statute-labour on the parish highways, is only loosely observed, and statute-labour is regarded more as a holiday and a means of begging alms from travellers than anything else. Over and over again the coach is surrounded by a swarm of such labourers, the King's Highwaymen, as they are called; one of your fellow-travellers suggests that the King's Loiterers would be a better name.

So your journey continues. Occasionally the coach shakes and jolts, rumbling like a cannon, over the cobbles of some narrow-streeted, evil-smelling town, but such are few and far between. Once on a lonely stretch of road one of the axle-trees breaks, and you have to wait some hours till it is mended. The last time he travelled to London, a lawyer in the company tells you, the coach overturned twice so that all his fellow-passengers fell on top of him and strained the joints of his leg, while on another occasion the traces broke and the horses went on, leaving them all sitting in the middle of the road.

The worst part of the journey is on the third day when you travel through the region of heavy midland clay, where the road between Biggleswade and Baldock is so bad that the coach is forced to break through a hedge and take to the fields to avoid the slough of despond between the hedges. The country-folk hereabouts are busy collecting tolls from travellers who are driven to this course. All this takes so long that the coach does not reach the inn at Baldock till almost midnight, and it is too late to get supper.

All through the fourth and last day of your journey
the sights of habitation and the concourse of travellers
increase. Everything seems to be converging on the
metropolis. Every half-mile or so, a cloud of dust
proclaims a drove of cattle, hogs, sheep, or geese,
winding in a long column towards the London
slaughter-house which is the lodestar of their poor
lives. Here the roads are a veritable quagmire, sodden
with the ordure of this never-ceasing procession of
doomed beasts, and you are forced to stop your nose to
avoid the smell.

For the last hour or two of the afternoon the scene
again changes, and you cross a desolate lonely upland
with scarcely a house in sight. The guard loads his
pistols and you peer anxiously at the clumps of bushes.
For here on wild Finchley Heath is the most perilous
stage of all your journey—the haunt of the London
highwaymen. Here every fellow-traveller is an object
of suspicion, and a group of cloaked horsemen coming
up over the brow of a hill just ahead causes a regular
panic. But it turns out to be a troop of dragoons who
are on the look-out for a gang who robbed a great
Lord's coach only this morning, a few hundred yards
from this very spot.

Just before sunset you turn a little out of the main
stream of traffic and climb the long ascent to Highgate.
Here, across a belt of two more miles of green fields,
you can see the towers and spires of London, now
rising again after the great fire of twenty years before,
and far off by the river a forest of masts. Then, as it
grows dark, the streets close about you and the hoofs
and wheels rattle on the cobbles. To your country ears
the noise is like the roaring of the sea: endless faces peer
into the coach and the rich smell of crowded humanity

assails your nostrils. Tired and bewildered as you are, it is all immensely exciting. All of a sudden there is a tremendous scraping and groaning and the coach is stuck fast in a narrow street between the stone posts on either side. It is too dark by now to extricate it, and, stiff and dazed, you clamber out. There is nothing for it but to leave your luggage with the guard till morning and walk to your inn. A crowd of beggars, clutching and mumbling, surround you, a ragged link-boy appears with a flaming torch to escort you, and, with your fellow-travellers and a bundle of hastily gathered belongings, you set out through the London lanes to finish your journey on Shanks's pony.

9

Wellington's Most Audacious Battle

This is he that far away
Against the myriads of Assaye
Clash'd with his fiery few and won.

Tennyson

FIFTY YEARS before I was born, and within the memory
of men and women with whom I have spoken, there
was to be seen, walking or riding the London streets, a
most distinguished-looking old man. Wherever he
went, everyone stopped and saluted as though he were
a king. As men uncovered, he would lift a stiff
forefinger to the brim of a tall grey hat. The gesture was
never omitted and never varied. He was always
immaculately dressed, in spotless white trousers and a
skin-tight, single-breasted blue frock-coat. His hair
was silvery, his eyes bright and piercing, his figure lithe
and upright as a boy's, save for the shoulders which
were bent with age, his finely chiselled features and
long Roman beak like an eagle's. To the early
Victorians he seemed as much a landmark as St. Paul's
or his own gigantic statue—cocked-hat, cloak, world-
famous charger—riding above the triumphal arch
opposite his house at Hyde Park Corner. Everyone
called him the Duke, as though, in a country with two

dozen of the richest dukes in the world, there was only one.

As long as Wellington lived, for most Englishmen there was only one. Yet he was a simple man—bleak, frugal, unsparing of himself. As his contemporary, Greville, wrote, he was without a particle of vanity or conceit. Though surrounded by admiring crowds whenever he appeared, he never seemed aware of the universal adulation. He did whatever he was asked to do by the Government of his day; took, as Greville said, 'more pride in obeying than in commanding, and never for a moment considered that his great position and elevation above all other subjects released him from the same obligation which the humblest of them acknowledged. An ever-abiding sense of duty and obligation made him the humblest of citizens and the most obedient of servants. The Crown never possessed a more faithful, devoted and disinterested subject.'

Thirty years before, at the age of forty-six, he had performed the greatest miracle of the age. For ten hours, until the arrival of the Prussians, he had held the ridge at Waterloo with a largely raw, untrained, and unco-ordinated international army against a veteran French force twice its size in real effectives and commanded by the greatest military conqueror of all time. His Prussian allies, badly beaten at Ligny two days before, were a day's march away, and Napoleon had staked everything on forcing a victory before they could reach the field. But for the Duke there is no doubt he would have done so. It was Wellington's calm, inflexible will, his brilliant dispositions and control of his slender forces, above all the tremendous prestige of his past victories, as he rode, immaculate and unperturbed, along the stricken ridge, that kept his young troops to the sticking-point until, as night fell, the furious French attacks weakened and collapsed and the Prussians came up.

Yet the Duke had not always seemed a hero to his countrymen. Fifteen years after Waterloo, the hated champion of a lost political cause he had been booed by the rough mob of the unpoliced capital whenever he appeared in the streets. His house in Piccadilly still carried the iron shutters—it does to this day—which he had had installed in front of the gaping windows the populace had smashed while his dead wife lay inside. This time he had been unable to hold the political ridge with his handful of peers and Tory diehards, and the Whig and Radical forces of Reform had swept victorious across it. Yet in defeat and retreat his calm greatness had become once more apparent. The principle on which he acted, then as always, was his own undeviating ideal of duty. The King's government, he said, must be carried on; civil war—the worst of all evils—avoided; the public served. For this end he was ready to sacrifice everything: Party consistency, reputation, his own pride. The only thing he never broke was his word and his honour. He led his forces off the field and continued to serve the State in subordinate, as in supreme, office, and with the same unsparing devotion. He was the greatest public servant—and soldier—Britain had ever known.

Twelve years before his final battle at Waterloo, Arthur Wellesley, as he then was—a Lieutenant Colonel of thirty-four in the English Army List, and a newly gazetted Major-General in that of the British East India Company—won a battle in the summer of 1803 against odds as great in real terms as those which Clive had faced at Plassey half a century before, or Henry V at Agincourt in 1415. His countrymen, who at that time were volunteering in their thousands in every corner of their threatened island to defend it against Napoleon's Grande Armée—then encamped on the cliffs above Boulogne—knew little or nothing of what was happening in their vast and remote Indian dependencies, a six months' voyage away. And when, five years later, Arthur Wellesley's name first became known to them it was as a cautious Fabian General and master of defensive warfare, precariously campaigning on the Atlantic fringes of the Iberian peninsula, lately overrun by the all-conquering legions of Napoleonic France.

It had been the appointment in 1798 of Arthur Wellesley's brilliant and ambitious eldest brother, Lord Mornington, as Governor-General of the British East India Comany's scattered dominions in India, that had given the young infantry colonel—a younger son of an impoverished Anglo-Irish nobleman—his first opportunity of command in war, of which his only experience until then had been a disastrous British retreat across a frozen Holland in the winter of 1794, and of which he afterwards said, 'I learnt what not to do, and that is always something.' It was Mornington's resolve to make Britain the paramount power in an anarchical India which, in the opening years of the nineteenth century, gave his younger brother the chance to show of what he was capable. A realist without romantic illusions, and set to administer part of Mysore in the south-western part of the vast oriental peninsula, Arthur Wellesley had quickly grasped that the way to govern a people long used to being ruled only by the sword and the plunderer was to ensure them security for life and property, and respect for native beliefs and customs with a scrupulous observance of every promise and undertaking given them. The crying need of cultivator, craftsman, merchant, and landowner was public order and justice. It was not the function of the soldier, Wellesley held, to conquer wider territories, but to suppress lawless violence: in Virgil's words, to impose the way of peace, spare the subject, and battle down the proud. On the army's ability to do this for India and its people of all creeds, castes, and classes, British rule must rest. 'It depends,' he wrote 'on justice, freedom from corruption, and unswerving truth to one's word and to every obligation one has undertaken.'

In pacifying and establishing order in a land where anarchy was endemic Wellesley also learnt that success in Indian warfare depended on meticulous organisation of commissariat and transport. Only through this was it possible for small forces of regular, disciplined troops to hunt down, starve into surrender, and disarm far larger, light-footed, and rapid plundering armies. 'How true it is', he wrote on one occasion, after a swift-footed adversary had escaped through a last-minute failure of his own supplies to arrive in time, 'that in military operations time is everything.'

Following the collapse in the eighteenth century of the great conquering Moslem empire of the Moguls, and with the British as yet firmly established only in their three coastal Presidencies of Bengal, Madras, and Bombay, the arbiters of central India were the marauding armies of Mahrattan horsemen who, under robber dynasties of usurping military adventurers, kept all eastern and central Hindustan in a state of perpetual turmoil. One of their greater chieftains, Madajee Scindia, had recently occupied Delhi itself—

the old Imperial capital—holding the heir of the Moguls a puppet-captive there. With their clouds of fierce irregular cavalry and their infantry and artillery officered and trained by French mercenaries—for long Britain's principal European rivals in India—the Mahrattas, when united, were a match even for the East India Company's disciplined Sepoys, if not for the tiny handful of Regular English and Scottish regiments which the British Government loaned to the Company. By their perpetual plundering they had reduced vast areas to starvation and made the life of the Indian cultivator a misery.

It was to tame their power that in 1803—on the renewal of the war in Europe between Britain and Revolutionary France—Lord Mornington, set on bringing the Mahratta power under control and closing the last door to French intervention, called on his soldier-brother to move a Sepoy army of ten thousand men, with its ordnance and supplies, from south-western India to the British Bombay province on the borders of the Mahratta military princedoms. And to do so across six hundred miles of a bridgeless, anarchical land where there was no law, no civil government, and where the cultivator was at the mercy of roaming bands of plunderers.

In war against the Mahratta princes—with their European trained infantry and massive artillery, a far more formidable enemy than the vast disorganised rabbles of unreliable native mercenaries whom Clive had routed half a century before—regular supplies in the field were essential. Otherwise, hordes of irregular Mahratta horse could drive any assailant into a position where he could be surrounded by their vastly superior numbers of infantry and then be annihilated by massed artillery. 'They follow him with their cavalry in his marches,' Wellesley wrote, 'and surround and attack him with their infantry and cannon when he halts, and he can scarcely escape from them. That, therefore, which I consider absolutely necessary in an operation against a Mahratta power ... is such a quantity of provisions in your camp as will enable you to command your own movements and to be independent of your magazines.'

This was the end to which all his immense organising powers were directed. 'If I had rice and bullocks', he recalled long afterwards, 'I had men, and if I had men I knew I could beat the enemy.' In past Indian campaigns enormous quantities of hired bullocks had to be used by the British, necessitating hordes of attendants and camp-followers, all of whom had to be fed, so reducing the army's rate of advance to a bare five miles a day. And the appalling consequent wastage of animals through inefficient handling, shortage of fodder, disease, and starvation had meant that, when the siege-train and its heavy guns reached their destination, there were never enough bullocks surviving to bring them back, and they had had to be left where they were and abandoned.

Arthur Wellesley's answer to this was to rely on a 'public' bullock department whose personnel were employed by the Company under regular supervision and discipline, only hiring additional draught-cattle when it was necessary, on monthly contracts with strict penalties for failure—based on prompt payment, 'which ought', he wrote, 'to prevail in all the Company's transactions with the natives of this country.' As a result, in a countryside which had been heavily plundered by a marauding Mahratta armies, he was able to cover the six hundred miles from Seringapatam to Poona in the worst season of the year without the loss of a single draught-animal and at an average rate of thirteen and a half miles a day. Once during his two months' march, his ordnance and provision train travelled sixty miles in thirty hours—something which in past Indian wars would have been impossible.

Wellesley covered the last forty miles in a single night at the head of four hundred horse. By gaining the confidence and co-operation of the lesser Mahratta chieftains along the line of march, and by the admirable discipline he maintained, with a resultant complete absence of plunder, he completed the transfer of his army from southern to central India without the slightest opposition. The far-reaching political consequences of his great march, a colleague considered, were due to 'the admiration which the southern Mahratta chiefs entertained of his military character and the firm reliance the inhabitants placed on his justice and protection.'

He had now, however, to deal with the great northern chieftains, Dowlut Rao Scindia, Maharajah of Gwalior, and Ragojee Bhoonslah, the Rajah of Nagpore, now styling himself by the even grander title of Rajah of Berar—a vast territory including regions recently filched from Britain's ally, the Nizam of Hyderabad. Together they could put into the field, against Wellesley's troops from Mysore and the Company's subsidiary division from Hyderabad, some 50,000 men, or more than three times the joint British forces opposed to them. Their plundering armies, with those of their fellow Mahratta, Jeswunt Rao Holkar, Maharajah of Indore—who, however, for the moment was glutted with the plunder of the Peshwah's lands—dominated all Hindustan. Scindia's resources were very great, and he and Ragojee Bhoonslah between them controlled most of central India. Wellesley still hoped to avoid open war with them, believing that, if Britain remained firm but concilia-tory, their threats would end in nothing. For, holding that India's trouble lay in lack, not excess, of native authority, he had no wish, like his brother, to destroy their independent rule, but merely to make it peaceful and responsible.

It soon became clear that Scindia and the Rajah, with their vast marauding host massed on the northern territories of Hyderabad, were merely playing for time. Having been given plenary powers by the Governor-General to expel them either by diplomacy or war, after prolonged negotiations and repeated warnings to them to withdraw Wellesley delivered a final ultimatum on 6 August. 'I offered you peace', he wrote, 'on terms of equality honourable to all parties; you have chosen war and are responsible for all consequences.'

For though he could look for little aid from his Indian allies, the Nizam of Hyderabad and the Peshwah, who failed to provide the grain they had promised and refused to admit his troops, even the sick, into their fortresses, he had made his usual careful provision for keeping the field. Every detail down to the minutest point of equipment and transport had been anticipated. Even before leaving Seringapatam, he had arranged for a new depot on the Bombay coast, to which, as he marched towards it, he transferred his maritime base by an imaginative use of sea-power which anticipated by a decade his brilliant 1813 Peninsular campaign. Here he established vast supplies: thousands of cattle for slaughter, salted meat, biscuits, and arrack for his European troops, rice for his Indian, and grain for his horses, with medical stores of bark, Madeira, mercurial ointment, calomel, and nitrous acid. Using his public bullock-train—'good cattle, well driven and well taken care of'—to keep his army provisioned in the field, his plan was to advance north-eastwards into the interior to join the Company's Hyderabad contingent which, under its commander Colonel Stevenson, was trying to prevent the Mahratta army from striking deeper into the Nizam's territories. Then, with the united Army of the Deccan of some fifteen thousand British and Sepoy regulars and several hundred native auxiliary horse, he intended either to force the superior enemy to battle or keep them so closely on the run as to make it impossible for them to plunder, thus depriving them of the only resource by which so large a body could be kept in the field. And, by equipping his forces with boats and pontoons to enable them to cross flooded rivers during the rainy season, he hoped to steal a march on an enemy dependent on fords. 'Keep your infantry in a central situation and let your supplies collect them', he advised Stevenson, who was anxious on account of the width of front he was having to hold till his chief could join him. 'Move forward yourself with the cavalry and one battalion, and dash at the first enemy that comes into your neighbourhood. You will either cut them up or drive them off . . . A long defensive war will ruin us . . . Dash at the first fellows that make their appearance and the campaign will be your own.'

Wellesley's first step was to secure a firm strategic base for his drive into the interior. Marching from Poona, he laid siege on 8 August to the great Mahratta fortress of Ahmednuggar, a place of immense natural strength which had often before been attacked, but never taken. On the first day he carried the town wall or pettah by storm, following it up with the capture of the main fort two days later. 'Those English', wrote an astonished eyewitness, 'are a strange people and their general a wonderful man. They came here in the morning, looked at the pettah wall, walked over it, killed all the garrison and returned to breakfast! What can withstand them?'

By the capture of the fortress Wellesley had secured an impregnable advanced-depot and communications-centre. 'I shall fill Ahmednuggar with provisions', he announced, 'and when that is completed all the Mahrattas in India would not be able to drive me from my position.'

For he had no intention of standing on the defensive. With a speed and daring comparable to that of Bonaparte in his recent Italian campaigns, he was out to break the arrogant Mahratta confidence. 'We must get the upper hand,' he wrote, 'and, if once we have that, we shall keep it with ease and shall certainly succeed.' To do so he relied on his three British regiments, with whom he believed he could achieve almost anything, so indomitable was their spirit and so great their ascendancy in morale. In a report written after the campaign, he paid a tribute to their qualities:

They are the main foundation of the British power in Asia. Bravery is the characteristic of the British Army in all quarters of the world, but no other quarter has afforded such striking examples of the existence of this quality in the soldiers as the East Indies. An instance of their misbehaviour in the field has never been known; and particularly those who have been for some time in that country cannot be ordered upon any service, however dangerous or arduous, that they will not effect, not only with bravery but a degree of skill not often witnessed by persons of their description in other parts of the world.

I attribute these qualities, which are peculiar to them in the East Indies, to the distinctness of their class in that country from all others existing in it. They feel that they are a distinct, and superior class to the rest of the world which surrounds them, and their actions correspond with their own notions of their superiority. Add to these qualities that their bodies are inured to climate, hardship and fatigue by long residence, habit and exercise to such a degree that I have seen them for years together in the field without suffering any material sickness; that I have made them march 60 miles in 30 hours and afterwards engage the enemy, and it will not be surprising that they should be respected as they are, throughout India ... These qualities are the foundation of the British strength in Asia ... They show in what manner nations, consisting of millions, are governed by 30,000 strangers.

And they were 'as orderly and obedient', he added, 'as they are brave.'

In his immediate command Wellesley had two Highland regiments—the 74th and 78th Foot—and one English regiment of horse, the 19th Light Dragoons. On 24 August, after a halt at Aurungabad, his Army of the Deccan crossed the swollen Godavery river in basket-boats made of bamboo laths, thorn, and leather—a device for campaigning in a bridgeless land which he had copied from Caesar's *Gallic War*. Linking forces with Colonel Stevenson's Hyderabad division, he began to shepherd Scindia's and the Rajah's harrying hordes northwards and eastwards, seeking every opportunity to bring them to battle without giving them a chance to escape the hunter's net and double back to plunder the Nizam's or Peshwah's territories. All the while, marching sometimes by day and sometimes by night, and making a fortified camp at every halt—another lesson learnt from Caesar, whose *Commentaries* and the Bible were the only books he took with him on the campaign—his men kept up a steady three miles an hour, measuring the day's march by the perambulator or measuring-wheel which always accompanied his Indian marches. 'I never was in such marching trim', he told John Malcolm on 6 September. 'I marched the other day 23 miles in 7½ hours . . . It is impossible for troops to be in better order.'

On 22 September he and Stevenson, now more than two hundred miles from his base on the Bombay coast, temporarily separated, each taking a different defile through a range of hills barring their way, both to save time—for the passes were too narrow for both to use simultaneously—and lest, by leaving either open, their quarry might slip through and fall to plundering again in their rear. It was arranged that they should join forces again on the 23rd and attack the enemy next day, if he had not by then retreated again.

But when on 23 September Wellesley emerged from the hills, with Stevenson still ten miles from the rendezvous where they were to camp for the night, he was informed by his native guides that the Mahrattas were starting to retire and that the cavalry had already moved off, leaving the infantry and guns to follow. The opportunity of catching the latter strung out on the march was too tempting to miss, and he at once decided to attack without waiting for Stevenson. Owing to the enemy's immense strength in cavalry, it was impossible to confirm the accuracy of the report without using his whole force to reconnoitre. But when, moving forward to attack the, as he thought, retreating foe, he found that he had been grossly misinformed, and that the whole Mahratta army of more than forty thousand men was drawn up in battle array on a six-mile front immediately in his path, their infantry and artillery on their left behind the steep-banked Kaitna river, and the cavalry on the right and moving up fast against him.

His position was most precarious. Threatened by an overwhelming deluge of native cavalry, it was impossible to stand where he was and be attacked in an unprepared position by an enemy six times his strength with more than a hundred guns to his own fourteen, with eight light pieces. Yet, if he fell back on his fortified camp and waited for Stevenson, he would be harried by the hordes of horsemen already swarming round him and might well lose his baggage-train, already under fire, and, with it, all further mobility of movement and chance of catching his quarry. Without hesitation he decided to do the one thing which could both secure his outnumbered force from destruction and simultaneously enable him, by rolling up the Mahratta infantry from the flank, to achieve the aim of his offensive. For if he could destroy them, the war would be won, since only a hard-core of disciplined infantry and artillery, such as Scindia's French officers had trained, could enable the traditional Mahratta cavalry hordes to subsist in face of the fast-moving, self-contained field-forces he had created for their discomforture and destruction.

Feeling, therefore, that the opportunity might never recur, he staked everything on being able to traverse the enemy's front and find a passage across the river somewhere beyond their extreme left from which vantage-point to turn back and assail them. He had, he told John Wilson Croker many years later, some of the best native guides that could be had, and he had made every effort to ascertain whether the river was anywhere passable, though all his informants had assured him that it was not. He resolved therefore to see the river for himself, and accordingly, with his most intelligent guides and an escort of cavalry, he pushed forward to a small eminence opposite the village of Assaye, which stood beyond it and on the bank of another stream, the Juah, running nearly parallel. There he again questioned his guides about a passage, which they still asserted not to exist. Yet he could see through his spy-glass, a short way beyond the enemy's left, one village on the near bank of the Kaitna and another exactly opposite it on the other bank. So, the account he gave Croker continued, 'I immediately said to myself that men could not have built two villages so close to one another on opposite sides of a stream without some habitual means of communication either by boats or a ford—most probably by the latter. On that conjecture, or rather reasoning in defiance of all my guides and information, I took the desperate resolution, as it seemed, of marching for the river, and I was right.' 'I found a passage, crossed my army over, had no more to fear from the enemy's cloud of cavalry, for my army, small as it was, was just enough to fill the space between the two streams, so that both my flanks were secure.' Yet though the passage of the ford was not contested, a battery of guns opened up a heavy fire on his troops as they crossed, and there were a number of casualties, including Wellesley's own orderly dragoon who had his head carried off by a cannon-ball— the terrified horse, with the headless body still in the saddle, scattering his staff as they splashed their way to the far bank.

By a stroke of richly deserved fortune, Wellesley thus gained the vantage-point he was seeking. Yet in doing so he had deliberately placed himself in a position of even greater peril. His left, as he had foreseen, was guarded by the river he had forded and his right by the tributary stream, the Juah, running parallel to it. But before him was an enemy far stronger than himself, and with an overwhelming superiority in artillery, and, behind him were two unbridged rivers with the Mahratta cavalry holding the far bank of the only ford. And, though he had placed himself, as he had intended, on the Mahrattas' flank, they had, with their recently gained skill in manœuvring, quickly changed front on perceiving his passage of the river, and were now drawn up between the Kaitna and the Juah with more than a hundred cannon and at least fifteen thousand foot, including sixteen battalions of French-trained infantry. His own seven thousand appeared doomed.

It is doubtful if in any battle of modern times a responsible commander ever took a more daring calculated risk to achieve victory. In none even of the young Napoleon's battles had there been anything quite to equal it. Wellesley had no advantage in weapons such as was enjoyed by British commanders in later Indian wars; in cannon he was hopelessly outnumbered. Except for his three British regiments—a mere fifteen hundred men—there was little to choose in morale and discipline between his fine Sepoys and the valiant Mahratta infantry and gunners. But like the great admiral Nelson, who five years earlier had shattered the French fleet in Aboukir Bay and was now, at that very moment, once more at his station off Toulon, Wellesley had taken every conceivable care to ensure victory. And, now that the chance had come, heavy though the odds might seem, he was ready to stake everything on it. He knew that in battle with the Mahrattas—the bravest and fiercest fighters in Hindustan—the only safe rule was to attack first and never give them time or opportunity to use their superior numbers to encircle, and then, with their cannon, to annihilate. He knew, too, that taught by their French instructors the new Revolutionary tactics of using masses in dense columns under cover of intensive artillery bombardment, Scindia's infantry and gunners constituted a more formidable force than any encountered in the Indian battles of the past. A few weeks earlier he had been warned of their new-found fighting skills by the Company's former Resident at Scindia's court, Colonel Collins, then on his way back to Bombay—a little man with a flash of fire in his dark eyes, looking in his antique military coat and black silk hat crowned by an ostrich feather, 'not unlike a monkey dressed up for Bartholomew Fair.' 'I tell you, General,' he had said at the end of their interview, 'their infantry and guns will astonish you.'

'In all great actions there is risk', Wellesley had written a few weeks earlier to his brother, the Governor-General. The wise course in action, he once said, is to attack your enemy at the moment he is preparing to attack you. In front of the little British-Sepoy force the confined space between the two rivers seemed to one who was present 'to be covered by one living mass to which our handful of men . . . was but a drop in the ocean.' Preparatory to attacking, Wellesley drew up his infantry in two lines behind a low ridge which partly sheltered it from the enemy, with one of his two British regiments, the 74th Highlanders, on the right, and the other, the 78th Highlanders, on the left, and with the cavalry as reserve in the rear. Yet even in this position the fire of the Mahratta artillery was so intense that to remain exposed to it would be suicide, and, though his troops had already marched twenty miles under a burning sun since dawn, he ordered an immediate advance. Warning the officer commanding the pickets in front of the 74th to avoid the strongly held village of Assaye on the enemy's left, where their heavy batteries were concentrated, he himself directed the main attack against their right along the banks of the Kaitna through what he described in his despatches as 'a very hot fire from cannon, the execution of which was terrible.' 'It seemed', wrote Captain Blakiston of the Honourable East India Company's Engineers, 'as if each individual felt that this was to be the test of discipline against numbers and that nothing but the utmost steadiness and determination could make up for the appalling disparity of force . . . Not a whisper was heard through the ranks; our nerves were wound up to the proper pitch, and everyone seemed to know that there was no alternative but death or victory.'

But while on the left flank Wellesley succeeded in his object, forcing back the enemy's infantry from the Kaitna and driving them, a congested mass, towards the Juah, on the right his little army was faced with disaster. For his brave picket commander, Colonel Orrock, in the storm of smoke and fire lost his sense of direction and led his men and the 74th Highlanders, who were following, straight into the mouth of the batteries massed around Assaye. 'In the space of little more than a mile,' wrote Blakiston, 'a hundred guns, worked with skill and rapidity, vomitted death into our feeble ranks.' In one platoon all but seven out of fifty men fell. Reduced from a battalion to little more than a company and still desperately defending its colours, the 74th was simultaneously assailed by the fire of the massed cannon in Assaye, the musketry of Scindia's French-trained infantry, and a fierce charge of Mahratta horse. After losing seventeen officers and nearly four hundred men, the Highland regiment was only saved from annihilation by Wellesley sending in his cavalry reserve to their rescue. In a magnificent charge the 19th Light Dragoons and the Fourth Native Cavalry not only routed the Mahratta horse but drove the enemy's first line of infantry into and across the Juah.

Gradually, in the furious hand-to-hand mêlée of the assault, the tide of battle turned as the British second line came into action. Everyone in Wellesley's little force distinguished himself; in the Eighth Native Infantry, known as 'Wellesley's Own', five officers and non-commissioned officers of one famous fighting family all fell. Wellesley himself refused to blame the officer whose mistake in leading his men and the 74th into the hell of fire around Assaye occasioned at least half his casualties. 'I lament the consequences of his mistake,' he wrote in his dispatches, 'but I must acknowledge that it was not possible for a man to lead a body into a hotter fire than he did the picquets on that day against Assaye.'

'Clashed with his fiery few and won.' Throughout the engagement the thirty-four year-old commander never weakened in his resolve to break the enemy's will to resist. He himself had one horse shot under him and another piked, while almost every member of his staff was struck down or had his mount killed. He was described by one young officer of the 78th, Colin Campbell, whom he had made a brigade-major for his gallantry at the storming of Ahmednuggar, as being in the thick of the action the whole time: 'I never saw a man so collected as he was', he wrote. Many years later his Spanish aide, Alava, recalled how in battle Wellington became a man transformed—'like an eagle.' He can never have seemed more so than on this desperate field. At one moment a havildar of native cavalry, who had captured a Mahratta standard, was brought to him for congratulation, at which—'with that eloquent and correct knowledge in the native language for which he was celebrated', recalled Sir John Malcolm—he promoted him on the spot with the words, *'Acha havildar; jemadar.'* Long afterwards, when the victor of Assaye had become world-famous, at a dinner attended by his old comrades-in-arms to commemorate his victory, the Indian soldier whom he had honoured on the battlefield, and who looked back to it as the greatest moment of his long and honourable life, could not be persuaded to speak of his former commander as the Duke of Wellington, saying that that was his European name, but that his Indian name was 'Wellesley Bahadur'—Wellesley the Invincible!

The day was finally won in the gathering dusk when the Highlanders carried Assaye with the bayonet, driving the enemy from their guns, ninety-eight of which remained in their hands. It was, the victorious general reported, the most severe battle he had seen or, he believed, that had ever been fought in India. It showed 'what a small number of British troops can do.' Close on half had fallen, and more than nine hundred of the Sepoys and native auxiliaries. But the enemy's casualties were four times as great, and they had lost almost every gun, while Scindia and the Rajah had fled the field. 'I believe such a quantity of cannon and such advantages have seldom been gained by any single victory in any part of the world', Wellesley wrote to his brother, the Governor-General. Once, in old age, when asked what was the best thing he had ever done in the fighting line, he was silent for a while, then answered, 'Assaye.' He did not, said his interrogator, add a word.

10

Green Land Far Away

'A' babbled of green fields.'
Shakespeare

TWENTY-FIVE YEARS after Wellingtons's culminating victory at Waterloo, he was still in 1840, after reaching a hale and sprightly three-score years and ten, the most celebrated spectacle in a London over which, exactly a century later, the Battle of Britain was fought. Capital of the wealthiest and most powerful nation on earth, from its Parliament beside the Thames, Britain directed the destinies of more than a tenth of the world's twelve hundred million inhabitants. Since the East India Company's little British and Sepoy Army had broken the Mahratta power at Assaye in 1803, Britain had extended her rule over the whole of an Asiatic peninsula thirty-four times the size of England, bringing nearly half its two hundred million multi-racial Indian inhabitants under her direct rule and the remainder, still governed by native princes, under her virtual control. An even vaster area of North America, inhabited by a sprinkling of British and French settlers and indigenous Red Indians, acknowledged the sovereignty of the Crown, and, at the other side of the world, separated from England by a six months' sea voyage, a newly discovered continent nearly forty times her size. Scattered about the world were other countries, large and small, ports and islands which flew the British flag—one on which, it was said, the sun never set.

In all this vast global dominion, there were only at that time two million men and women of British race outside the British Isles, apart from the garrisons of the little Regular Army which, being purely voluntary, was far smaller than that of any other major Power. It was Britain's complete mastery of the seas—won by the Royal Navy during the past century and a half in seven successive wars between 1689 and 1815, which, culminating in the defeat and exhaustion of her rival and neighbour, France, with a population nearly three times her own, had given her an unchallenged ascendancy over the world's ocean trade routes.

The continent of Europe, of which Britain was geographically—though not politically—a part, consisted of thirteen Christian nations, a Mohammedan and partially Asiatic Ottoman Empire in its south-eastern corner, and forty-one minor German and Italian states which, though enjoying sovereign independence, lacked national status. Four only were major Powers: the restless French, formerly revolutionary but since restored Bourbon and Orleanist, kingdom with thirty-five million inhabitants—a source still of perpetual fear to its neighbours; the old multi-racial Hapsburg Empire of Austria with a slightly smaller population; the parvenu north German military Kingdom of Prussia with sixteen millions; and the vast semi-barbaric Empire of Russia with more than sixty millions, of whom seven millions inhabited the

Siberian Asian plains. The once powerful Kingdom of Spain and the Ottoman Empire, still exercising an uneasy and despotic sway over the semi-Christian tribesmen of the Balkans, no longer played any part in the councils of Europe.

Of the other continents, Africa was a savage *terra incognita* with a fringe of decadent Mohamedan states littering its Mediterranean shore—one of which, piratical Algiers, had recently been annexed by France—and a few scattered British, Dutch, and Portuguese outposts along its ocean coasts. Round the latter passed the sailing ships which carried the trade of Europe to the East. Asia, with more than two-thirds of the world's population, had become a European trading preserve, though still largely unexploited, with its southern peninsula British, its vast northern deserts Russian, and only the moribund Empire of China preserving a semblance of loose independence, while British traders and gunboats injected western commerce and culture into her eastern ports and creeks. Japan was a group of dreamy islands, still unopened to European trade and innocent alike of western idealism and material progress.

Only in North America was there any civilisation comparable to that of Europe. Here seventeen vigorous millions, still mainly of British descent, who had broken with the too rigid rule of Westminster sixty years before, were engaged in developing and throwing open to European emigration an only partly inhabited continent. In central and southern America, seventeen scantily populated and ramshackle Latin and half-Indian states, recently revolted from Spanish and Portuguese rule, offered an almost illimitable field to the capitalist and industrialist trader and exploiter.

Here also Britain, with her sea-power and manufacturing and banking supremacy, was first among trading rivals.

The population of England and Wales, now some fifty millions, in 1840 scarcely exceeded fifteen. That of Scotland numbered another two and a half million, and Ireland—a restless half-subject state—a further eight millions or nearly twice what it became after the terrible Irish potato famine of 1846 and the consequent mass emigration to America. Of these twenty-six millions, including two millions living in London and another million and a half in seven new industrial cities of over a hundred thousand inhabitants, scarcely more than a quarter lived in towns of over twenty thousand. The rest dwelt, as their fathers before them, among the fields or in towns from which the fields were only a few minutes' walk. At least half the British race were engaged in rural or semi-rural pursuits. The overwhelming majority were the sons or grandsons of farmers, yeomen, peasants, and domestic craftsmen.

With its two million inhabitants, London, by far the largest and richest city in the world, like the nation itself had more than doubled its population since the beginning of the century. Stretching from Shadwell and Wapping in the east, it extended along both banks of the Thames as far as rural Chelsea and Battersea; thence a double line of villas, ensconced among trees and large gardens, continued almost to Hampton Court. For the first time in its history the city was venturing away from the river; houses, skirting the new Regent's Park to the north, strayed into the fields and farms of Primrose Hill where children still gathered the flowers which gave it its name. Everywhere bricks and mortar were continuously rising: the removal of the Court from St. James's to Buckingham Palace had stimulated an outburst of building on the marshy fields and market gardens of Pimlico, soon to be renamed after its Cheshire owners, Belgravia. The red brick of which Wren and his successors had re-created London after the great Fire of 1666 was everywhere giving place to white and potentially grimy stucco:

> Augustus at Rome was for building renowned
> And of marble he left what of brick he had found;
> But is not our Nash, too, a very great master,
> He finds us all brick and leaves us all plaster.

Standing on top of the Duke of York's column on an early summer day of 1842, the downward-glancing eye lighted on a jumble of old houses and red-tiled roofs mingling with the foliage and blossom of Spring Gardens. Along the Mall the trees still straggled anyhow, unregimented into their modern columns, while cows thrust their horned heads over the wooden palings of Carlton House Terrace. Trafalgar Square was building on the recently cleared site of the old Royal Mews, where untidy advertisement-pasted hoardings concealed the stump of Nelson's slow-rising column and the Percy lion, with its straight poker tail, roared defiance above the Tudor brick palace of the Dukes of Northumberland. Farther afield loomed the great Pantechnicon in Belgrave Square, and Apsley House, with its world-famous inhabitant and its ferruginous shutters defying reform and revolution, standing solitary against the country setting of Hyde Park. Beyond lay Kensington village and the first rising mansions of Bayswater. Southwards near the river, by the Abbey and the long straight line of Westminster

Hall, Barry's new Houses of Parliament were still only rising from the scaffolded ashes of old St. Stephen's. Opposite that empty spot stood the eighteenth-century houses of Bridge Street and Westminster Bridge; beyond tall chimneys, bespeaking the industrial employments of the dwellers in the Lambeth and Southwark suburbs, and the virgin heights of woody Penge and Norwood.

This city, multiplying itself in every generation, was still governed on the rustic model of its own past. Side by side with the medieval Lord Mayor and Corporation were three hundred parish and other authorities, mostly Vestries, whose functions overlapped in the most inextricable manner and whose members, self-elected or holding office for life under no less than 250 Acts of Parliament, interpreted democracy in their own jovial way by almost ceaseless entertainment at the public expense. The hammering and plastering that daily enlarged London's circumference went on without control or interference: except for the new west-end squares which Cubitt was raising for the Marquis of Westminster, the small speculating builder built as he felt fit. It was the age of 'superior Dosset', carrying his yeoman frugality and peasant notions of propriety into the building of a new Rome. Nobody had time or money to plan: there were no broad avenues or boulevards; the town, free from continental fortifications, grew outwards not upwards and on the principle that the best place to build was the nearest available space. The brand new suburbs which housed the City clerks over the former village pastures and gardens of Islington, Hoxton, and Camberwell, were monotonous agglomerations of mean streets and terraces marked by pathetic Cockney attempts at gentility and country ways of living wherever there was room for a vine, a carpet-sized flower garden or a fanlight over the narrow hall.

That was the new London; it was still overshadowed by the old. Past the great white invitations to 'Try Warren's' or 'Day and Martin's Blacking' and the castellated summer houses and villas of the outer bourgeoisie, the traveller entering London felt the shock and heard the roar of the cobble-stones and saw elm trees and winkle stalls giving way to continuous lines of houses and gas lamps. The narrow streets through which the coaches and drays forced their way were thronged with the human material from which Dickens and Cruikshank derived their inspiration. Women in fringed shawls and straw bonnets, pock-marked and ragged beggars and pickpockets, clean-shaven and tightly stocked young men with mutton-chop whiskers and tall fluffy beaver hats, clerks, also crowned with the universal stove-pipe, flowing in-wards to the counter or back to suburban villages—'preceded by a ripple of errand boys and light porters and followed by an ebb of plethoric elderly gentlemen in drab gaiters'—and, as one reached the fashionable squares and roadways of Mayfair, a wealth of coloured and gilded liveried servants with stuffed white calves, cockaded hats, and gold aigulets, emulating prize cattle in their rotund solemnity. These not only mixed with the crowds on the pavements and appeared sunning themselves at innumerable doorways but flowed majestically along the streets at a higher level, as they sat red-nosed on the draped boxes or stood erect with tall silver-crowned canes on the swinging platforms of crested coaches. And behind the double doors of the great houses of Grosvenor Square and Piccadilly were their brethren, the hall porters, sitting in vast hooded chairs, sometimes with a foot-rest and a foaming tankard as witness of their master's absence in the country.

These were the rank and file of the private armies of the privileged, sleeping in truckle beds in tiny dusty attics or dark basement pantries but sharing their master's glory and living on the cream of the land. At the great routs of High Society and at the Levées of St. James's, the populace crowding about the flambeau-lit doorways could see them in all their magnificence, enacting their well-rehearsed parts in the cavalcade of the last age in which the English rich expended their wealth on public pageantry instead of on personal comfort. The bedizened flunkeys and the elegant, disdainful beings they attended never lacked spectators: a nimbus of ragged wide-eyed urchins, somtimes jeering, always half-admiring, attended them wherever they went—gamin school and spawn of the true Cockney with his love of splendour and his delight in derision.

Here the ages mingled—the past and the future. The great country houses of Piccadilly behind their high stone walls, ignoring London and dreaming of the shires from which the rosy country-bred lords and legislators who governed England hailed, were washed by the creaseless tides of the London of commerce. Jogging past those tall brocaded eighteenth-century windows, the fathers of the Forsytes sat crowded and upright within or sprawled, long-legged and check-trousered, on the narrow knife-edged roofs of the little sixpenny buses that, driving a resolute way among the crested barouches, chariots, and landaus of the fashionable west-end, plied between the Bank and

outer Paddington and Brompton or the Yorkshire
Stingo close by leafy Lisson Grove. At the back, straw
in his mouth and ribaldry on his lips, stood the
outrageous cad, loudly touting for passengers against
the conductors of rival machines and pushing his
clients through the narrow door into his hot, swaying
straw-strewn pen. There they sat, six aside on the
dirty plush cushions, glaring suspiciously while their
thoughts ranged ahead of the steaming horses on
schemes of money-making which never troubled the
fine pates of the great lords and ladies whose residences
they were humbly passing. For in the first days of the
young Queen new England was on the make and old
England was on the spend. The nation's growing
wealth offered scope for both.

Looking back across all the eight decades of our own
century and the long prosperous reign that preceded it,
we know how vigorously and inevitably that young
England was advancing to victory, how doomed was
the antique pomp and stately polity it supplanted. At
the time the battle seemed undecided: the foundations
of the old world looked firm and brassy and the busy,
vulgar confusion of the new rootless and evanescent.
The teeming legions of the money-makers were there
on sufferance: back in the shires from which they or
their fathers came, they paid the common immemorial
tribute to the lords of hereditary status and acre. Down
in his native Wessex by the sea, superior Dosset, master
of London bricks and mortar, touched his cap with his
yeoman cousinry to the squire of Lulworth or
Osmington. Here in London he fought for a footing in
a crowded hurly-burly from which status was lacking
for all but the richest. Even for his place in the
omnibus—the advancing chariot of democracy—he

had to rise betimes and struggle: for in the race for money, many were called and few chosen and the prize was only to the assiduous, the pertinacious and the thrifty. In 1837 London only boasted four hundred narrow, three-windowed, two-horse buses and twelve hundred dirty hooded gigs or cabs, with a total carrying capacity of less than ten thousand.

Other public conveyances there were none. The river, whose scourings the tides could be no longer cleanse, had ceased to be the city's waterway: the watermen who had ferried the generations of the past between the stone stairs were dying out. Mostly, London tramped over the cobbles to its labour, nearly a hundred thousand pedestrians daily crossing London Bridge. In those narrow crowded streets Shanks's pony generally proved the swiftest mount: with long swinging strides the Londoner covered his morning and evening miles and went abroad for country rambles after his midday Sunday dinner. The studious Macaulay thought nothing of walking for recreation from his chambers in the Albany to New Cross or riverside Greenwich.

It was a London that still had a country appetite. It ate not because it wanted vitamins but because it was hungry. At midday the new London sat down in a panelled steaming chop-house—at 'Cock', 'Rainbow', or 'Cheshire Cheese' and many a humbler horse-box hostlery—to devour steaks, joints, chops and porter, cheese, potatoes and greens, usually with hot spirits and water to follow. Off liver and bacon at 10*d*., a pint of stout at 4½*d*., potatoes, bread, cheese, and celery one could dine very comfortably for 2*s*. and leave a pile of coppers for that loquacious piece of old England, the waiter. Men whose immediate forbears had been hale and hearty farmers would think nothing of tackling at a sitting a boiled leg of mutton with carrots, turnips, and dumplings, black pudding of pigs' and sheeps' trotters, tripe and faggots and pease pudding. In their appetites the gentry were at one with the rising commercial classes: at Lord Grey's house Creevey sat down with five or six others to a luncheon of two hot roast fowls, two partridges, a dish of hot beef steaks, and a cold pheasant, and to a 'double' dinner of two soups, two fishes, a round of beef at one end of the table and a leg of mutton at the other with a roast turkey on the sideboard, followed by entrées of woodcocks, snipes, and plovers, with devilled herring and cream cheese to lay the last despairing stirrings of appetite. Dinner was followed, after due time allowed for the gentlemen's port, by tea, and, where late nights were in contemplation, by the supper tray—Melton pie, oysters, sandwiches, and anchovy toast with sherry, bottled stout, and Seltzer-water and the usual mahogany case with its four cut-glass decanters labelled Rum, Brandy, Whisky, Gin. The London poor, few of whom tasted butcher's meat more than once a week, had to content themselves with envying the well-filled forms and rosy faces of their betters.

The poor—the flotsam and jetsam of casual labour and the ne'er-do-wells who lacked the status and solider fare of the skilled artisan class—were somewhat of a problem in that great city, and the bigger it grew the more of them there were. The magnet of wealth seeking more wealth drew them from the dissolving world of status and the hedgerow, and from the old trades which the new were paralysing. To house them the jerry builders worked ceaselessly, raising innumerable straight streets of plain two-storied houses with

slated roofs, the cheapest that could be built. Here, and
in the regions where older and grander buildings had
decayed to verminous tenements, they lived and died
and multiplied, for despite filth and cholera and typhus
life proved stronger than death. Even the down-and-
outs and the homeless urchins, sleeping in their
thousands under the arches of the Adelphi and
Waterloo Bridge, lived.

Many of the worst slums jostled the dwellings of the
rich and the haunts of fashion. There were rookeries of
thieves and prostitutes under the very noses of the
lawyers in the Temple and the legislators in Westminster, and close behind the fine new plate-glassed shops
of Regent and Oxford Streets the urban poor squatted
in worse than farmyard filth and squalor. But few
troubled much about the poor who were left to the
Vestries and Providence: every one was too busy
making money or spending it. Only sometimes a
wretched creature, rising from the shadowy recesses of
London or Waterloo Bridge, would mount the parapet
and, sliding into the water, take swift dramatic leave of
a world that knew small pity for failures.

Strangely contrasted, the life of rich and poor yet
mingled. In Tothill fields, the scholars of Westminster
took almost daily part in gigantic battles against gangs
of young roughs from the adjoining slums. And the
street-walkers on their promenade from Temple Bar to
Westminster Hall knew more of the good and great
who ruled the aristo-democracy of England than the
good and great would have cared to admit. Many of the
traditions of the Regency died hard, paying tardy
deference to the more squeamish and frugal morals of
the money-makers. Fine gentlemen of the shires,
accustomed of ancient use and lusty living to take their

pleasure of the willing wives and daughters of their tenantry—and no one, in their estimation, the worse in thought or fact—kept dual establishments in town: a house in Portland Place or Berkeley Square for family and *haut ton* and a pretty box for some charmer, promoted from ballet or millinery shop, in one of the little Chelsea or Brompton Squares that were ever rising on the sites of the western market gardens. At night the young bucks and their hangers-on would assemble at the Cavendish or some neighbouring Piccadilly hostlery. When the white damask was strewn with empty jugs of Château Margaux and broken decanters of port, they would sally out to wrench off the knockers and bell-handles of Sackville Street and Vigo Lane, make merry with the blackguard democracy of the London underworld on comic songs, roast kidneys, cigars, and gin and water in the smoky haunts of Leicester Fields and the Haymarket, and finish the night in riotous harmony amid the dishevelled Cyprian delights of the Piccadilly Saloon, or at Vauxhall Gardens, watching the fireworks and the dances in the Rotunda from a leafy grotto and lingering long into the morning over sliced ham and a bowl of arrack with the nymphs of the place. The sleepy turnpike men on the Bridge and the newly formed Metropolitan Police, in their tall hats and clumsy belted coats, treated such privileged revellers with respect so long as they kept their amusements from assuming too dangerous a shape. The 'Peelers' had been brought into the world not to molest but to protect property and its owners. For on the untrammelled use of property, it was held, the nation's liberties depended.

A rough natural democracy governed by an aristocracy and landed gentry was the English model with plenty of scope for folk who wished to be free and easy. But already the shades of a more prim and decorous age were falling: the new police and the new passion for making laws had begun to trace on the nation's ruddy face the sober lineaments of a more formal society. In Oxford Street the first wood blocks had already taken the place of the cobbles, and in the larger thoroughfares the stone posts on the pavements were being crowned with spikes to discourage the urchins of the streets from their interminable leapfrog. The day-long music of the London street cries was beginning to grow fainter.

Within the club-houses of Pall Mall and St. James's, a new life for the rich, based on decorum and silent comfort, was taking the place of the noisy gambling and drinking of the unregenerate past. By 1837 there were twenty-five of these great institutions from behind whose windows warm men with broad acres or money in the Funds could sit over their *Quarterly* or *Edinburgh Review* and watch a safer and remoter world than their fathers had ever known. Here the old and the new were already learning to mingle, and the successful man of commerce who had negotiated the terror of the black ball might hope to strike an acquaintance with the quieter sort of lord or squire. There was even a special club dedicated to Reform with the most famous chef in London installed among tin-lined copper pots and gas ovens to teach old England the way to live after a new French model.

At night the march of progress was symbolised by the lighting of the London streets. Gas lighting had come in a couple of decades back, and was now being slowly extended from the main thoroughfares into the courts and alleys of the older London that besieged them. The great gasometers rose like fortresses above the drab rows of working-class dwellings, and from dusk till dawn the flaring gas jets made a peculiar humming that was the musical background to the nocturnal activities of the Londoner. Judged by modern standards the light they gave was dim and little defused: to our rustic forefathers it seemed a prodigious illumination. Yet four years were to elapse before the main road from Hyde Park Corner to Kensington was lit by a single lamp.

The essential services of life were still supplied to the Londoner after a country model. Donkeys carried vegetables to Covent Garden and colliers or 'Geordies' brought their 'best Wallsend' from Tyne and Wear by sail: a prolonged west wind could cause a fuel shortage in the capital. And the wintry streets were perambulated by tall-hatted coalheavers peddling their wares. Here, too, the old cries of London were still heard: in winter crossing-sweepers sat by braziers to gather toll of familiar clients for keeping their pitch clean. In her rough white cottage in Hyde Park opposite Knightsbridge, old Ann Hicks sold gilt gingerbreads and curds and whey and took her modest toll, won by half a century of prescription, of Park brushwood and hurdles to make her fire. In the new Bayswater road one could watch haymakers in the open fields to the north: a little farther on, where the gravel Oxford turnpike fell into Notting Dale, the pig-keepers who supplied the London hotels squatted in rustic confusion. In the cellars of Westminster as well as in the suburbs Londoners still kept cows: the metropolis' milk supply was mainly home-made with, so it was hinted, liberal assistance from the pump. And on any

Monday morning herds of cattle were driven by drovers armed with cudgels and iron goads through the narrow streets to Smithfield: pedestrians were sometimes gored by the poor beasts. In Smithfield Tellus kept his unsavoury rustic court: a nasty, filthy, dangerous country Bastille in the heart of London and a great offence to sensitive and progressive persons. Vested interests defended it stubbornly against all assaults: *Punch* depicted a proprietary Alderman taking his wife and family for a walk there. 'Oh! how delicious', he declares, 'the drains are this morning!'

How rustic London still was could be seen from its summer greenery. The west-end was full of trees and green squares and courts. The fields were half a mile away from Buckingham Palace and Grosvenor Square, and snipe were occasionally shot in the Pimlico marshes. In St. James's Park long rough untrimmed grass ran down to the water's edge, and there were no railings to keep people from wandering on it. Sometimes on wintry evenings the scarlet of a huntsman's coat could be seen in the fading light ascending the slope of Piccadilly or entering the Albany courtyard.

In Chelsea, where the old brown roofs and twisted high chimneys of the houses almost tumbled into the unembanked river, the sage Carlyle rode down eighteenth-century lanes to improve his digestion. Here on Saturdays would come bowling by many 'a spicy turn-out and horse of mettle and breed', with the little liveried top-hatted tiger swinging on the footboard behind and his gay bachelor master smoking his cheroot and flicking his whip as he sped to his riverside villa, with its fairy-like grounds, cellar of recherché wines, pictures, statues, and 'many a gem of vertue.'

Elegant London of royal Victoria's virgin days where Jullien, the Napoleon of Quadrille, 'saucily served Mozart with *sauce-piquant*' and Taglioni danced like a spirit in Rossini's newest ballet! For all its ragged hungry urchins, its fever-stricken alleys and crushing poverty, there was still music and gaiety in it. In August 1842, Mozart's *Cosi fan tutte* was being sung at His Majesty's and Rossini's *Semiramide* at Covent Garden under the direction of Benedict, while Purcell's *King Arthur* was rehearsing at Drury Lane and Spohr's new opera, *The Fall of Babylon*, at the Hanover Rooms.

There was a pastoral quality about the amusements of our great-great-grandparents. The summer regattas on the Thames between London Bridge and Hammersmith were attended by paddle-steamers with brass bands and boats full of fluttering flags and pretty girls giggling in the sunlight under painted awnings, while the banks were thronged with runners and riders and convivial parties watching from the festooned balconies and gardens of riverside pubs. At Putney Fair were Fat Ladies and Learned Pigs, much 'firing of cannon, jollity, shouting, jangling of street pianos and popping of ginger beer,' and many a pull at Finch's ale. Every Whit Tuesday the Cockneys went *en masse* to Greenwich, cargo after cargo going down the river singing and cheering and devouring stout and sandwiches, to sample the traditional delights of the great fair—its rows of booths hung with dolls, gilt gingerbreads, and brandy balls, its raree-shows and performing pigs, its giants and its dwarfs. Here prentices and shop boys pushed about with whistles, penny trumpets, false noses, and rolled twopenny scrapers—in sound simulating tearing material—down the backs of their elders. And the park was filled with young people and hoydens—playing at kiss-in-the-ring, riding donkeys, or, more simply, tumbling head over heels down the hill.

For though London was the greatest city in the world its people still had their roots in the country or were separated only by a generation or two from country ways. They were scarcely yet sophisticated. The poorer streets were frequented by gigantic brown dancing bears led by picturesque, seedy-looking Italians. Barry, the clown at Astley's Circus, went down the Thames in a washing tub drawn by geese, and a lady rider at Vauxhall could draw all London. For children the chief sights of the town were the Tower, the Elgin Marbles, and Mr Cross's Surrey Zoo, recently moved from the old Royal Mews to make way for Trafalgar Square. Here in the grounds of Walworth Manor lions and tigers perambulated in a circular glass conservatory more than a hundred yards wide and a giant tortoise carried children on his back. Another popular treat was the Panorama. At the Colosseum on the east side of Regent's Park one could view the Fire of London with canvas scenery and fireworks and the Alps with a real Swiss and a real eagle. Athens and the Himalayas were also shown for a shilling—'the Ganges glittering a hundred and fifty miles off, and far away the snowy peak of the mountain it rises from.' A little later a new Royal Panorama was opened in Leicester Square, where scenes from England's contemporary colonial wars were presented in the manner of a newsreel. The battle of Waterloo—the chief title-deed, with Trafalgar, of an Englishman's innate superiority to all foreigners—was a permanent exhibit.

For sport the well-to-do Londoner affected the pastimes of squires and farmers. Cricket was already established at Lord's suburban ground and was played vigorously in top-hats: but shooting parties, steeple-chases, hunting with the Queen's, the Old Berkeley, or the Epping Hunt, and fishing up the river were far more widely patronised. At Richmond the well-to-do merchant and shopkeeper, arrayed in top-hat, white tie, and long tail coat, would sit in a punt of a Saturday afternoon perched on a chair with rod and line, dining afterwards at the Star and Garter and calling on the way home at the pastrycook's to buy his wife six-penniworth of Maids of Honour. The Englishman, though immersed in low commerce, liked above all to think of himself as a man of potential acres—a younger son who might one day come into his heritage. His, as R. H. Mottram has written, was 'that almost divine snobbery of very strong motive power that keeps the Englishman from being content ever to be classed as a workman or labourer, a priest or soldier or scholar, as men of other civilisations are, and makes him always desire to be a gentleman, a word without equivalent in any other language.'

The old Chelsea bun house, the ale-house standing solitary in the Kensington road between Hyde Park Corner and the royal gardens, the ox that was roasted whole in the park on Coronation Day, were all reminders that the capital of a great empire had not wholly shaken off the village. So were the established bad characters who frequented its shady gambling-houses and saloons, the imitation bucks and dandies, the bankrupts, bullies, and half-pay captains who still, in the last age before the railway came in, sometimes emulated Macheath and Turpin by robbing the benighted traveller in Epping Forest or on the Surrey heaths. On an execution morning at Newgate one saw the rough old London of the landless squatter—greasy, verminous, and grimy—gathered outside the gaol; ribaldry, coarse jokes, reckless drinking, and un- ashamed debauchery continued uproariously until the chimes of St. Sepulchre's striking eight and the tolling of the prison bell brought a momentary hush as the prisoner mounted the steps and the sickly jerk of the rope gave the signal for an unearthly yell of execration. For countrymen deprived of their land and status soon degenerated.

So rough and ill-disciplined was that London that until Home Secretary Peel had established his Metro- politan Police in 1829, St. James's Park had been patrolled by Household Cavalry. Many still living could remember the terrible week when the mob, emerging from its filthy lairs in the cellars and crazy tenements of Blackfriars and St. Giles's, had sur- rounded Parliament and all but burnt the capital. When in the winter before her coronation the little Queen, with pretty pink cheeks and pouting mouth, drove behind her emblazoned guards through the streets, the crowd gaped but scarcely a hat was raised or a cheer heard. 'The people of England', wrote Greville, 'seemed inclined to hurrah no more.' Even at Ascot in the following summer only a few hats were raised as the royal barouche drove down the course.

There were some in that age who thought England was driving to a republic. For a hundred and fifty years the innate English loyalty to the monarchic principle had been undermined by the iconoclastic Whig contempt for royalty and its pomps and gewgaws, by a family of foreign rulers on the throne and during the last four decades by the vagaries and indecorums of the royal family. Since the death of Charles II, the royal England of Elizabeth and the Plantagenets had been transformed almost unknowingly into an oligarchy. Though the dignity with which the young Queen bore her part in the ceremonies of coronation in the summer of 1838 did something to stir deeper and latent national instincts, the general feeling was expressed by William Dyott when he wrote, 'A very young Queen coming to the throne of this mighty empire (just eighteen years of age) brought up and subject to the control of a weak and capricious mother, surrounded by the parent's chosen advisers . . . gives token of unpropitious times to come.'

The real rulers of England were still the greater squires. They were the most accomplished and cultured aristocracy the world had ever seen: by their great houses and avenues, their libraries and noble possessions and their likeness limned by Reynolds or Gainsborough, one can see the manner of men they were. They left their mark on English literature and art as the Athenian aristocracy did on that of ancient Greece—a mark that was both lovely and imperishable. They increased the wealth and power of their country beyond measure, extended her dominions into every sea, gave her arts and industries that enriched the human race for generations, and confronted by superior force, humbled by their inspired use of English courage and manhood the tyranny alike of Grand Monarque, Revolutionary Tribune, and military Empire.

They had almost untrammelled power; they gambled, hunted, drank, and whored, they feared no man, they did what was good in their own eyes, yet they did it with some measure of moderation and restraint. In this they differed from other tyrants and were like the ancient Anthenians. By the time our chapter of English history begins, they were already past their prime and starting to decline. One sees them in the tell-tale pages of Mr Creevey: with their rentals multiplied out of all measure by improved agriculture and urban expansion, but already divorced by their staggering wealth from that close contact with reality and their humbler fellow-citizens which had enabled their forebears to obtain power. Their ruling passion was the chase. Their tragedy was that they were getting spoilt by their own excessive wealth and power.

Such men were cold in their Olympian calm and detachment; passionate like all their countrymen in their robust vitality and the intensity of their personal feelings. Aristocratic statesmen reproaching one another on the floor of the House did not at times restrain their tears: and a burst of momentary indignation could create life-long and unappeasable enmities. In 1828, Wellington, then Prime Minister, fought a duel because a fellow-peer in the heat of political controversy had charged him with Popery. Lord George Bentinck was reported to have lost £27,000 in a single race: Jack Mytton—climax of English aristocratic eccentricity—went out for a bet stark naked on a winter's night to shoot duck and drank a bottle of port before breakfast. The breed was as vigorous in its loves as in its hates and wagers: another Prime Minister was cited as co-respondent in the Divorce Courts when approaching the age of sixty. A great lady in her eighties, asked by her son-in-law when a woman ceased to feel passion, replied, 'you must ask a woman older than I am.' Intellects were as tough as passions; strength, natural and quite unconscious, was the distinguishing mark of the race.

Even at its worst—and sometimes in men like the Marquis of Hertford, Thackeray's Lord Steyne, and Disraeli's Monmouth, it was very bad indeed—the standard of that aristocracy was bound up with a sense of *noblesse oblige*. They were landowners and they were hereditary legislators, and as both they had traditional duties to perform which they felt they could not leave undone without shaming themselves and their caste. The Duke of Rutland', wrote Greville,

is as selfish a man as any of his class—that is, he never does what he does not like, and spends his whole life in a round of such pleasures as suits his taste, but he is neither a foolish nor a bad man; and partly from a sense of duty, partly from inclination, he devotes time and labour to the interest and welfare of the people who live and labour on his estate. He is a Guardian of a very large Union, and he not only attends regularly the meetings of the Poor Law Guardians every week or fortnight, and takes an active part in their proceedings, but he visits those paupers who receive out-of-door relief, sits and converses with them, invites them to complain to him if they have anything to complain of, and tells them that he is not only their friend but their representative at the assembly of Guardians, and it is his duty to see that they are nourished and protected.

His fellow Duke of Richmond made it his business to visit the sick-room of the Workhouse of which he was Guardian when cholera and typhus were raging among the inmates: he had been in the army, he said, and did not fear these contagions.

The English aristocracy and the country gentry ruled by virtue of the fact that they were the focus on which the national society centred. Wherever they were so—in the village, in the small country town, in London—their position seemed strong and assured. Wherever that focus was lacking—in the great industrial cities and on the absentee estates of dispossessed Ireland—aristocracy was already in eclipse and decay. But it still kept a substantial measure of its ancient hold on the mind of England. In its salons in London the intelligentsia were still welcome: middle-class Mr Macaulay might talk 'like ten parrots and a chime of bells' but he took his place by right of intellect among the beeches and princely patronage of Bowood and in the rooms of Holland House. 'The world has never seen and never will see again', wrote Greville, 'anything like Holland House.' In that society almost everybody who was conspicuous, remarkable or agreeable was expected automatically to bear a part.

The instrument of authority through which the landed classes governed was the House of Commons. Since the seventeenth century, the greater landowners had preferred to rule through the lower House in preference to their own. In this they showed unconscious wisdom, since those set in authority over the English usually in the end provoked their jealousy and incorrigible sense of independence. The power of the nobles, established over the Crown in 1688, had been preserved by being concealed. Throughout the eighteenth century the Lords did little more than record the decisions of the Commons. But they exercised their authority by their control of the electoral machinery of the old unreformed Parliament and by the presence of their relations and dependents in the lower House. Before the Reform Bill, the Duke of Buckingham alone is said to have controlled the votes of a dozen members of the House of Commons. Such a man had as much parliamentary power as that of a great city like Manchester.

The Reform Bill of 1832 broke this power. Henceforward it was not the landed magnates of England who controlled its urban franchise. They still continued to wield considerable interest, both through their presence in successive Governments and through their family and social ties in the House of Commons. In Lord Melbourne's Whig Cabinet of 1835, eleven out of fourteen members were lords or the sons of lords: in its Tory successor of 1841 nine. But ultimate power was soon to pass into other hands—to the voters of the growing cities and towns of industrial England.

Not that anyone yet realised it. The £10 householders enfranchised in 1832 scarcely constituted a revolutionary body. They were a respectable and to those of superior station who troubled to approach them rightly, an even deferential body, as the young Whig historian, Macaulay, deprived of Lord Lansdowne's rotten borough of Calne by the Reform Bill, discovered when he contested Leeds in 1832. 'My leading friends', he wrote to his sister, 'are very honest, substantial manufacturers. They feed me on roast-beef and Yorkshire pudding: at night they put me into capital bedrooms; and the only plague which they give me is that they are always begging me to mention some food or wine for which I have a fancy, or some article of comfort and convenience which I may wish them to procure.' The wealth, power, and culture of an ancient and complex community continued to be represented by those who possessed them. In 1840 nobody in

Parliament, and few outside, would have questioned the propriety of this.

Every few years a general election took place, and the party battle was then transferred to the constituencies. Here under the old unreformed system it had taken a form peculiarly English, with mobs processing through the streets with flags and banners, with party devices and mottos and special tunes—'Bonnets of Blue' for the Tories and 'Old Dan Tucker' for the Whigs—with companies of hired boxers and cabmen and paid toughs to intimidate the electors, with free beer and breakfasts at the expense of the candidate in every tavern, with the wooden hustings on which fine gentlemen who sought the suffrages of a free people grinned and suffered, while rotten eggs, oranges, and rude shouts whizzed over, under, and sometimes at, them.

This popular saturnalia, which was the special pre-rogative of the poorest and roughest elements of the community, served no apparent electoral purpose, for only a comparatively few quiet and well-conducted persons had possessed the vote, and elections were decided mainly by local territorial influence and the state of current opinion among the reading classes. But it served the ancient English purpose of letting off steam in a rough human way, and it helped to give uneducated people a sense that they were taking part in the government of the country without any of the disturbing consequences of their actually doing so. It gave a great deal of happiness and excitement, not to the rich and discreet, but to the uncalculating majority. It was becoming an increasing annoyance to respectable citizens of a liberal and reforming turn, who took every opportunity of attacking its abuses and trying to do away with it in the name of purer and more rational politics. For this reason, despite all its noise, roughness, and drunkenness, it was a dying institution.

From the bacchic tumult of the unenfranchised multitude which attended its election, Parliament itself was far removed. No boisterous breath of democracy would have been tolerated in the House of Commons which was still almost the most exclusive club in England. A number of northern manufacturers and eccentrics with radical hobby-horses were tolerated with humorous or contemptuous resignation by the well-groomed majority, who viewed them as they would have viewed the few old slovens and cranks at a fashionable public school.

The House was a place where the gentlemen of England sat or lolled at their ease, with feet stretched out before them, arms akimbo, and top hats tilted over their eyes or pushed comfortably to the back of their heads while papers and blue books were strewn idly on the floor before them. When, as often happened, the course of debate flowed languidly, many would stretch themselves out on the benches and sleep or watch the familiar proceedings of their House with half-closed eyes, some face downwards, others with legs in the air.

Honourable Members could not see anything incongruous in such a method of conducting their business: the House was as much their property as their own library or club, and to have questioned what they did there would have been the highest presumption. Only within the last few years had the right of the public to read first-hand reports of its debates in the press been tacitly admitted by the provision of a press gallery. Centuries of struggle and, more recently, of unchallenged supremacy had given the House its arrogant and serene assurance: the government was upon its shoulders and it carried the burden with nonchalance.

The gentlemen of England carried the same assurance into their administration of public affairs. 'Goose! goose! goose!' wrote Palmerston across a diplomatic despatch. The great Foreign Secretary treated what he regarded as the literary lapses of his country's representatives abroad like an outraged schoolmaster: one received back a despatch with an injunction that it was 'to be re-written in blacker ink', while another was forbidden to use the un-English gallicism 'corps diplomatique' and reminded that the expression 'to resume' did not mean 'to sum up' or 'to recapitulate' but to 'take back'. 'Sentences', he wrote on another occasion, 'should . . . begin with the nominative, go on with the verb and end with the accusative.' Such men were accustomed to leave no doubt as to what they meant in the minds of those they ruled.

In all this they represented, not inadequately, the people of rural England whose homely lands gave them their titles and wealth. They were rough and ready in their ways, brave and independent. Cock-fights and cock-shies, dog-fights, bull- and bear-baiting—though these were already dying out in most parts of the country—'purring' matches in Lancashire where men and women vied in kicking each other with clogs, bespoke the love of contest for its own sake that ran right through the nation. At Oxford sporting undergraduates, in ancient rooms lined with pictures of prize-fighters, race-horses, and dogs, would amuse themselves by opening a cageful of rats for their terriers to worry.

Boxing was the national sport *in excelsis*. Boys were brought up on tales of the classic exponents of the Science—of Tom Cribb, Gentleman Jackson, Gully who rose to the House of Commons, Mendoza, and Molineux the negro. Young noblemen had their pet prize-fighters: every village its 'best man', who had won his title in some Homeric contest with his predecessor. There were no Queensberry rules and men fought with their bare fists, sometimes to the death. In June, 1830, the Irishman, Simon Byrne, and the Scottish champion, Sandy McKay, met in the Buckinghamshire village of Hanslope: in the forty-seventh round the Scot fell unconscious to the ground never to rise again. His victor perished in the ring a few years later at the end of ninety-nine rounds.

Game to the death, such men bore little malice. Bad blood was not allowed to grow rancid: it was let after the fashion of the day on the green sward. A 'mill' brought all the neighbours running to see fair play and courage: afterwards the combatants were ready enough to be friends. There was something intensely good-humoured about that open-air, fighting England. It was rough but it was healthy. Borrow has left us a picture of an old prize-fighter, his battles over, keeping open house in his 'public' down Holborn way, 'sharp as winter, kind as spring . . . There sits the yeoman at the end of his long room, surrounded by his friends. Glasses are filled and a song is the cry, and a song is sung well suited to the place; it finds an echo in every heart—fists are clenched, arms are waved, and the portraits of the mighty fighting men of yore, Broughton and Slack and Ben, which adorn the walls appear to smile grim approbation, whilst many a manly voice joins in the bold chorus:

Here's a health to old honest John Bull,
When he's gone we shan't find such another,
And with hearts and with glasses brim full,
We will drink to old England his mother.'

The independence of the national type matched its pugnacity. For all the deference of traditional England to its superiors, it was a deference strictly based on established right and custom. It yielded little to claims based on anything else. A man owed certain duties to Church, State, and society to be performed according to his station: when they had been fulfilled, he owed no others. Lord Palmerston, in attendance as Foreign Secretary at Windsor Castle, rode as befitted his office beside her Majesty's carriage: when, however, she embarked on Virginia Water he did not accompany her but left the royal barge to row about in a dinghy, not choosing to miss his daily exercise. The skilled craftsmen of Birmingham disposed of their hours of labour in a similar spirit: when they had earned enough, they would take a day, or even a week, off to drink. Even the clerks of the Bank of England—though the new powers that were beginning to rule English society were fast taming them—insisted on their ancient rights of private trading and of receiving tips from clients, kept shops and pubs and drank spirits in office hours. For according to the old English reckoning a man who did his duty had a right to do it as he pleased.

Any interference by the State not established by prescription was viewed with abhorrence. This explains the ease with which the urban and radical doctrine of economic *laissez-faire* captured the mind of the older England. A magistrate told some poor pavement vendors, arrested by an officious policeman

for selling water-cress in Marylebone High Street, that
they had as good a right to sell their wares as other
people to dispose of anything else. When Income Tax,
abolished after the Napoleonic Wars amid the loudest
cheering ever recorded in the history of the House of
Commons, was reintroduced in 1842 at 7*d.* in the £ it
was regarded as an almost intolerable inquisition which
struck at the freedom and privacy of every respectable
Englishman. 'Private affairs must be divulged,' com-
mented a newspaper, 'private feelings outraged—
malicious curiosity gratified—poor shrinking pride, be
it never so honest, humbled and put to the blush—
deceit and the meanness of petty trickery, encouraged
in evasion—and much appalling immorality spread
with the abandonment of truth. Many a gentleman will
sicken over the forms he has to bear with; and many a
tradesman will become either ruined or a rogue.'

The more rustic the scene, the stronger this almost
exaggerated passion for independence. Fred Bettes-
worth, farmer's boy, wishing to see the world, left a
master with whom he was perfectly happy without a
word and waited on Staines Bridge till he found a carter
to give him new employment. A year or two later,
sooner than be tied, and feeling he had 'a kind o'
roamin' commission', he left another master and
tramped forty miles into Sussex to see the country.
Every summer for many years he did the same. In the
villages of Whittlebury Forest, almost every householder was a poacher: a decade or two back when the
gamekeepers of the enclosing lords had failed in the
face of local opinion to make an arrest for nutting in the
forest, the whole village of Silverstone had turned out
armed with staves to repel the Bow Street runners in
pitched battle and assert their ancient privileges. A

yeoman-farmer of the same place left a sum of money to cover his grave with spikes pointing upwards, swearing that he had never been trodden on when alive and would not be so when dead.

Such a type was well content with its own forms of life: it had no wish to oppress others but had small use for foreigners or their ways. At the Egham races William IV called out to Lord Albermarle to tell him the name of a passing dandy whose face was unfamiliar. Albermarle replied that it was Count D'Orsay. 'I had no notion it was,' replied the King: then, mustering all his energy, gave vent to the natural feelings of an honest English sailor in a loud 'Damn him.' 'If the French attempt to bully and intimidate us,' wrote the Foreign Secretary to the Prime Minister in 1840, 'the only way of meeting their menaces is by quietly telling them we are not afraid, and by showing them, first, that we are stronger than they are and, secondly, that they have more vulnerable points than we have.' And to the British Ambassador in Paris, the same organ voice of England spoke more expressly, 'If Thiers should again hold to you the language of menace . . . convey to him in the most friendly and inoffensive manner possible, that if France . . . begins a war, she will to a certainty lose her ships, colonies and commerce before she sees the end of it; that her army of Algiers will cease to give her anxiety and that Mehemet Ali'—the French protégé—'will just be chucked into the Nile.'

For, however uncritically, Palmerston saw himself and his country in the international sphere as the champion of the weak and helpless against the arrogant strong. 'As long as England', he declared in a famous speech in the House, shall ride pre-eminent on the ocean of human affairs, there can be none whose fortunes shall be so shipwrecked, there can be none whose condition shall be so desperate and forlorn that they may not cast a look of hope towards the light that beams from hence; and though they may be beyond the reach of our power, our moral support and our sympathy shall cheer them in their adversity . . . But if ever by the assault of overpowering enemies, or by the errors of her misguided sons, England should fall . . . for a long period of time, would the hope of the African . . . be buried in the darkness of despair. I know well that in such case, Providence would, in due course of time, raise up some other nation to inherit our principles, and to imitate our practice. But . . . I do not know any nation that is now ready in this respect to supply our place.

It was because it had so strong a sense of its own strength, sanity, and inherent decency that the England of character and tradition felt it had so little to learn of foreigners. Gladstone loved to tell the story of the dying Admiral who, when assured by his spiritual pastor of the glories of Heaven, cried out, 'Aye, aye—it may be as you say—but ould England for me!' The patriotism of the English was founded on their unbroken past. They felt themselves to be an historical people, 'generation linked with generation by ancestral reputation, by tradition, by heraldry.' The first Lord Redesdale in his *Memoirs* recalled an old peasant couple who lived in the tower of a ruined manor house at Mitford.

Their beautifully chiselled features, no less than their proud bearing and dignified manners, might have befitted the descendants of crusaders. She was always clad in an old-fashioned lilac print gown, with the square of shepherd's plaid crossed over the bosom. Her delicate, high-bred face, with blue eyes, still bright and beautiful, was framed in the frills of an immaculate mutch covering her ears and almost hiding the snow-white hair: her small feet were always daintily cased in grey worsted stockings and scrupulously blacked shoes. She must have been nearly eighty years old when I used to sit with her in her kitchen—the aged dame on one side of the hearth, the little boy on the other, listening to her old-world tales of the past glories of Mitford. There were always a few old-fashioned flowers in the kitchen parlour, and she herself sweetly reminded one of lavender. The good soul was always stout for the rights and honour of the family.

Such folk, like the old England they belonged to, were living on the momentum of a past tradition. It was now dying and in many places already dead. Its purpose had been to produce virtuous men and women. It had been rooted in the Christian morality of the medieval Church which, believing that the purpose of life was to save and prepare man's soul for Heaven, taught that wordly laws and institutions should be based as far as possible on the gospel of Christ.

A society founded on such principles did not, of course, succeed in establishing the rule of righteousness on earth. But it made it easier for the ordinary man to live a Christian life and taught him to revere just and honest dealing. When the corruptions inherent in the medieval ecclesiastical system resulted in the Reformation, the ideal of moral justice continued to haunt the English mind. For nearly three hundred years after the repudiation of papal authority, a Protestant but Christian Parliament, though with diminishing faith and vigour, continued to enact moral and sumptuary laws, to regulate labour and fix prices.

Yet, during the eighteenth century the momentum behind such paternal legislation had been fast running down. Among the intellectual leaders of the nation, faith in a divinely appointed order was giving way to a new belief in the unaided power of human reason. Men, it was felt, could live best, not by adherence to traditional standards of aggregate wisdom and justice, but by their own individual reason and wits. And with the weakening of the authority of the central government which followed the defeat of the Crown by the aristocracy, the rich and powerful grew restive at any interference with their own freedom of action. In every place where the old forms of organised life were giving place to new—in the capital, in the ports, and the industrial towns—the vigorous and stubborn Anglo-Saxon temperament, so tenacious for personal rights and jealous of freedom, responded to appeals to shake off the trammels of a feudal and priestly past.

Thus over an ever-widening circle the freedom and interest of the individual came to be regarded as more important than Christian justice and the community. In urban and commercial society the profit motive superseded the communal conscience as the ultimate arbiter of national society. Yet in the countryside where the old forms of an ordered life still lingered, there was an instinctive conviction, or prejudice, as some called it, that man was more important than money and moral health than reason. The State might divest itself of moral authority: but the individual conscience, moulded by unbroken centuries of Christian rule, remained. Whatever bagmen might practise and economists preach, the rural Englishman clung to an ideal which had nothing to do with profit-making and little with abstract reason—that of a 'gentleman.' He most valued the man whose word was as good as his bond, whose purse was ever open to the needy, whose heart was above calculation and meanness, and who was fearless towards the strong and tender and chivalrous towards the weak—in other words a Christian. When Squire Brown sent his son to Rugby, he asked himself before giving him his final injunctions what he wanted of him: 'Shall I tell him to mind his work, and say he's sent to school to make himself a good scholar? Well, but he isn't sent to school for that—at any rate, not for that mainly. I don't care a straw for Greek particles, or the digamma, no more does his mother . . . If he'll only turn out a brave, helpful, truth-telling Englishman, and a gentleman and a Christian, that's all we want.' A few years later, unconsciously answering his father's question, Tom defined his scholastic ambition as being, 'I want to leave behind me the name of a fellow who never bullied a little boy or turned his back on a big one.'

The forms of an organised religion, though increasingly neglected in the towns, helped to keep alive this noble temper in the country. In most villages the Church was still the centre of communal life; its Sunday service, with its gathering of the rustic hierarchy, churchyard gossip, and interchange of news, the chief social event of the week. Until the old string and brass choirs were superseded by the new-fangled organs and harmoniums, the village played almost as great a part in the exercise of communal worship as the parson. Standing each Sunday in the west gallery with their copper key-bugles, trombones, clarionets, trum-

pets, flutes, fiddles, and bass viol, these rustic in-
strumentalists represented a folk-tradition that was
older than squire or clergy. Yet for all their tenacious
clinging to old forms and ritual—'it allus has bin sung
an' sung it shall be'—the string choir was doomed and
the conservative democracy of the English village with
it. It was suppressed by the reforming vicar just as the
landed peasantry of the old unenclosed parish had been
by the reforming squire a generation or two before.
The effects of this iconoclasm were not yet fully
perceived; it took long to transform the habits and
character of a tenacious people. But the chain once
broken could not be repaired.

Already in many villages the established Church had
lost its hold on the rustic heart. Pluralism, though
recently abolished by ecclesiastical reformers, had long
accustomed country-folk to the spectacle of neglected
churches, perfunctory services, and clergymen who
seemed more interested in foxes and sometimes in the
bottle than the cure of souls. Left to themselves the
parishioners of such men lapsed into a strong native
paganism which, even in the age of faith, the Church
had never wholly eradicated. Every village had its tales
of ghosts and witches, of bygone murders and haunted
cross-roads and gibbets. Many of these old wives' tales
had a ring that went back to the past of fairy-lore and
border ballad:

> One lonely night, as I sat high,
> Instead of one there two passed by.
> The boughs did bend, my soul did quake,
> To see the hole that Fox did make.

Christian, as apart from pagan, faith among humbler
folk was by 1840 more often to be found in the

Methodist congregations which had spread like wild-fire through the countryside since Wesley's missionary journeys of the previous century as well as in the Baptist and Independent congregations of the older nonconformity. It was often of a somewhat primitive and uncritical kind but made up in fervour and homely force what it lacked in subtlety. Incidentally it had a stimulating effect on the Establishment, provoking a strong rivalry between 'Church and King' and 'Dissent'. To the adherents of the former the 'Methodies' were 'long eared 'uns'—ignorant and cantankerous fanatics—while to the Methodists, churchgoers seemed little better than damned. Yet even the most enthusiastic adherent of the meeting-house still preferred to be buried like his father in the churchyard. The historic community of the village was not quite dead.

Its dying flame burnt brightly at the traditional festivals of the Christian and pastoral year still kept in the countryside. At Christmas the mummers still came round to hall and farm-house with their age-long drama and unchanging characters—

> A room, a room, for me and my broom,
> And all my merry men beside,
> I must have room and I *wull* have room
> All round this Christmastide.

On Oak Apple Day the inns were decorated with oak boughs and the village lads wore oak apples in their buttonholes and cried 'Shickshack' to those who wore none. There were morris-dancers in duck trousers and white ribboned shirts and handkerchiefs at Whitsun, the summer Sunday School Treat when the gifts of home-brewed wine were divided by the teachers into two classes, the less alcoholic to be drunk by the children and the stronger by themselves when the children had gone to bed. Many villages had their annual Feast—a relic of the old pagan Whitsun Ale—when the lads and lasses out on service came home, the travelling fiddler appeared, the inns were crowded, and the Feast Ale tapped. Akin to it was the farm Harvest Home, eagerly looked forward to by many a hungry labourer, with its lit barns and groaning tables, its 'churchwardens' and beer jugs, its traditional songs—'The Jolly Ploughman', 'The Fox has gone through the Town O!', 'Poor old Horse'—and its crowning toast, 'Here's health to master and missus, the founders of this feast!'

The pride and patriotism which sprang from these things, however naïve and even pathetic they may appear to modern minds, attached not only to England but to every separate part of it. A countryman was thrice citizen of his country, of his shire, of his native town or village. All three were steeped in accumulated tradition and custom. The provincial capitals—York, Norwich, Exeter, Shrewsbury, Bristol—each had its own peculiar society, civic lore, and culture: its special crafts, domestic industries, and style of architecture, its cherished monuments and legends, its theatre, assembly rooms, and musical festival, its hereditary merchant and professional class and neighbouring gentry, and in some places such as Norwich even its own school of art.

The smaller towns and villages of England were as marked in their distinguishing differences. At Abbot's Bromley in Staffordshire on the first Monday after 4 September, the Deer Men with their hobby-horses danced the Horn Dance in painted reindeer heads and ancient costumes of red and green. In May, at the Furry

Festival at Helston, any person who would not join the dance and remained at work was set astride a pole and carried to the river there to leap or compound in cash for the good of the community.

> Where are those Spaniards
> That made so great a boast, O?
> They shall eat the grey goose feather,
> And we will eat the roast, O!

There was still a wonderful wealth and diversity in the local manner of celebrating the great Christian, and still older than Christian, feasts. On Christmas Eve in the villages of the New Forest libations of spiced ale were poured out to the orchards and meadows: at Huddersfield the children on their wassailing bore evergreens hung with oranges and apples:

> We are not daily beggars
> That beg from door to door,
> But we are neighbours' children
> Whom you have seen before.

> Call up the butler of this house,
> Put on his golden ring;
> Let him bring us a glass of beer,
> And the better we shall sing.

And after service on Christmas morning in many parts of the north country the whole people ran through the streets crying—

> Ule! Ule! Ule! Ule!
> Three puddings in a pule,
> Crack nuts and cry Ule.

In Wiltshire Shrove Tuesday was kept by bands of children marching three times about the churches with joined hands. In Suffolk the farm lass who could bring

home a branch of hawthorn in full blossom on May
Day received a dish of cream for breakfast. At
Polebrook, Northamptonshire, during the last days of
April, the May Queen and her attendants gathered
posies in the meadows and begged the loan of ribbons,
handkerchiefs, and dolls from their neighbours to carry
on garlanded hoops round the village to a song that
came out of the depths of antiquity. In other places
they sang:

> The life of man is but a span
> It flourishes like a flower,
> We are here to-day and gone to-morrow,
> And are dead in an hour.
>
> The moon shines bright and the stars give a light
> A little before it is day,
> So God bless you all, both great and small,
> And send you a joyful May.

All this betokened a culture founded not on Courts
and cities but on the green fields and the growing earth.
Like a tree it spread upwards. Walking among the
water meadows at Bemerton one could see its roots: the
spire of Salisbury Cathedral tapered skywards out of
the cup of the downs and the cottage-folk spoke of a
pious man named George Herbert whose grave was
forgotten but whose books they still read. In men's
hearts there dwelt a novel called the Past: its chapters
were their own earliest memories, hallowed by
repetition and loving association, and the tales their
fathers and the old wives of the village had told them.
  Like bees the country English gathered honey from
the flowers of their own history. The combs in which
they stored it were the manifold insitutions in which
they expressed their social life. Church and State were

only the greatest of these—prototype and symbol of all the others. Every parish was an institution—a living organism from which successive generations derived purpose and inspiration. When the parish bounds were beaten each year the whole community attended in witness of its own existence: the beer-laden wagons, the rough practical jokes, the unchanging rituals and chants were the shew-bread on the altar of Christian neighbourhood. A diary-keeping parish clerk records these homely pieties: 'stopt on the mount in the lane and cut X cross, put Osgood on end upon his head, and done unto him as was necessary to be done by way of remembrance . . . Old Kit Nation was turned on end upon his head and well spanked in the corner of Northcroft and upon the Wash.'

So, too, were schools and charities, walking by ancient beacons lit by the piety of men of old and tended by a long procession of successors. The Blue Coat boys of Christ's Hospital passed through the London streets in the belted gown of Edward VI's England and in the knee-breeches and shining shoe-buckles of that of George I; the children of the parish school of St. Botolph's Bishopsgate still wore silver badges and muffin caps. At Eton, under elms planted in the days of Charles I, the boys, celebrating the martial heroes of antiquity, kept the old feast of Montem—the tenure by which the College held its domains. All that human courage, quixotry, and goodness had achieved in the long sordid struggle of man against the stubborn forces of nature was, however crudely and imperfectly, treasured and commemorated as though to remind successive generations of their continuing heritage and nobler destiny. Few could see unmoved the heroic pageantry of the Trooping the Colour or the great annual spectacle of six thousand London Charity children assembled under the dome of St. Paul's, singing with that 'honest old English roughness that no man need feel ashamed of' while their eyes shone with the thought of the feast before them. As after the prayers thousands of glossy aprons fell simultaneously, it seemed to one watching like the fall of snow.

It was not only its own tradition that England celebrated, but those of the two great peoples of the ancient world—the Hebrew and the Greek—from whom they derived their cultures. Those who stood Sunday after Sunday in the parish church identified the songs and faith of Zion with their own rustic life. The manger in which Christ was born stood in the byre where the friendly beasts of the field crowded on wintry nights: the green pastures into which the Good Shepherd led his flock were the meadows of home. Men who could not write their names, but whose memories were unimpaired, knew every collect in the prayer book by heart and were as familiar with the Bible names as with those of their own fields. So for the more sophisticated the images of the classics were superimposed on those of their own England: an Eton boy recalled his first May Day walking by Fellow's Pond through a half-Grecian haze, 'the fairies tripping in rings on the turf, the dryads tempted out of their barken hiding-places, the water-nymphs making high festival on the silver flood.'

Knowledge of the classics was still a universal passport. It opened the doors of intellectual society. On that solid foundation of common effort and allusion, the culture of a gentleman rested. Statesmen quoted Latin in the Commons and even on the hustings: and busy men of the world found relaxation

in the evenings or on holiday in re-reading the authors
of the old pagan world whom they had first encountered at school or college. Macaulay defined an
independent scholar as one who read Plato with his feet
on the fender. In the characters of the ancient world
such men recognised themselves, their own failings and
virtues. 'I am reading Plutarch's lives,' wrote Edward
Fitzgerald, 'one of the most delightful books I have
ever read: he must have been a gentleman,' The
common experiences of life constantly recalled to such
readers the reflections of their fellow-men who had
passed the same way under other skies many centuries
before.

'I took down a Juvenal', one of them wrote to a
friend, 'to look for a passage about the Loaded Wagon
rolling through the Roman streets. I couldn't find it.
Do you know where it is?' The absorption of their
degenerate descendants in crossword puzzles and
detective novels is a faint and attenuated reflection of
this bygone passion. Sometimes the incongruity of it
struck them with a glow of pleasure: 'think', wrote one,
'of the rocococity of a gentleman studying Seneca in the
middle of February, 1844, in a remarkably damp
cottage.' Forty years later an English poet who had
grown up with the century, crossing Lake Garda on a
summer's evening, put into his native verse the innate
love of his generation for the classical learning of his
youth:

> Row us out from Desenzano, to your Sirmione
> row!
> So they row'd, and there we landed—'O venusta
> Sirmio'—
> There to me thro' all the groves of olive in the
> summer glow,

There beneath the Roman ruin where the purple
    flowers grow,
Came the *'Ave atque Vale'* of the Poet's hopeless
    woe,
Tenderest of the Roman poets, nineteen hundred
    years ago,
'Frater Ave atque Vale'—as we wandered to and
    fro
Gazing at the Lydian laughter of the Garda Lake
    below
Sweet Catullus's all-but-island, olive-silvery Sirmio!

The great country houses with the classical colon-
nades and porticos and their parks recalling some
gentle Sicilian or Thracian scene were a natural setting
for these gentlemen-scholars. Here the law of pri-
mogeniture afforded a nursery for the higher branches
of the national culture. Their library walls were lined
with the golden volumes of two centuries of English
and classical thought and learning: the child who grew
up in those stately rooms knew, subconsciously, that
he was heir to the ages. Even when, as often happened,
the eldest son abjured books for the superior charms of
horse, rod, and dog, it was almost certain that one or
other of his numerous younger brothers would acquire
in the freedom of his father's library the scholarly tastes
that he would carry into a wider world.

Here in the country-house was the accumulated
tradition not only of culture but of order. The life of a
great country-house afforded a microcosm of the state:
no fitter training-ground could have been devised for
those called upon by birth and wealth to rule. An
English landed estate in the first half of the nineteenth
century was a masterpiece of smooth and intricate

organisation with its carefully graded hierarchy of
servants, indoor and outdoor, and its machinery for
satisfying most of the normal wants of communal
life—farms, gardens, dairies, brewhouses, granaries,
stables, laundries, and workshops; carpenters, iron-
mongers, painters masons, smiths, and glaziers; its
kitchens, larders, and sculleries, beer and wine cellars,
gunrooms, and stores. At Woburn the Duke of
Bedford directly employed nearly six hundred persons,
three hundred artificers regularly paid every Saturday
night, and his bill for domestic pensions alone
amounted to over £2,000 a year. Here, Greville
reported, 'is order, economy, grandeur, comfort and
general content . . . with inexhaustible resources for
every taste—a capital library, all the most curious and
costly books, pictures, prints, interesting portraits,
gallery of sculpture, gardens, with the rarest exotics,
collected and maintained at a vast expense.' Almost
every county had at least one Woburn and a dozen or
score of hereditary mansions on a smaller but
comparable scale.

Such houses were the headquarters of what was still
the chief industry of England—agriculture. From their
estate offices a great national interest was directed.
During the past eighty years its productivity had been
immeasurably increased. New and revolutionary
methods of farming and stockbreeding had been
introduced and nearly seven million acres of waste land
reclaimed by enclosure. A German traveller in the
1820s was amazed on each successive visit to England
to see vast tracts of formerly uncultivated land
transformed into fine corn-bearing fields. It was during
these years that Tennyson's northern farmer was
engaged on his long and manly task of stubbing

'Thurnaby waäste.' It was all part of a tremendous national achievement. Though the population had doubled since 1760 and England had ceased to be a corn exporting country, more than three-quarters of its total wheat and nearly all its barley consumption were being met by the home producer.

By their agricultural activity and inventiveness the English had not only given an example to the world but saved themselves. The new methods of breeding stock, the increase of grazing, the use of fodder crops on lands formerly left fallow, fencing, building, and draining, contributed as much to the defeat of a militant and revolutionary France as the broadsides of Trafalgar and the stubborn squares of Waterloo. Without them the rising populations of the new manufacturing towns could never have been fed nor the power of Napoleon humbled. The accumulated experience of all this mighty effort had now been elevated into a science: the annual gatherings at Holkham to toast the great Coke of Norfolk who had turned thousands of acres of rabbit warren into a smiling countryside, the ceaseless output of books on improved methods of farming, and the foundation of the Royal Agricultural Society in 1838 were among its many symptoms.

One saw the industry in its corporate capacity on market day in any country town—the old market hall, the country women's stalls and baskets spread about the roadway, the gentry and tenant-farmers in their John Bull top-hats, loose open frock-coats, vast collars, white waistcoats and breeches, and heavy top boots. One saw it, too, in the great fairs that sprang up annually throughout the countryside, where a whole neighbourhood of peasant and farmer-folk would assemble to buy, gossip, and junket and when those who wished to be hired for service for the coming year proudly carried the symbols of their trade—the carter his whip, the milkmaid her pail, and the cook her ladle. The lads or lasses hired received a shilling as testimony of acceptance and stuck a ribbon in cap or hair in honour of the bargain. 'I took the shilling, put a bit of ribbon in mi' hat to show as I were hired like 'tuthers,' said an old farm labourer recalling the days of his strength and pride, 'and went and spent the rest of the day at the pleasure fee-ar.' And as night fell and the drums and bugles outside the painted, lit booths sounded over lonely down and far watching valley, the rustic fun waxed fast and furious. A national industry was relaxing.

It had its statelier moments. When Queen Victoria and her young husband came to Stowe in 1845, the farmers of the Bucks Yeomanry escorted the royal carriage from the Wolverton terminus, a cavalcade of five hundred of the Duke's mounted tenantry awaited them in Buckingham, and six hundred more in white smocks and green ribbons lined the avenue to the Corinthian Arch. That night delegations from all the neighbouring villages and from the county Friendly Societies waited on their sovereign with banners and torches, while the church bells pealed for twenty miles round and two thousand rosy-cheeked children sat down to feast in Buckingham town hall.

If the apex of the agricultural community and of its ordered industry and culture was the country house, its basis was the cottage. It was here that those who reaped and sowed were born and bred. Their homely virtues were as vital to their country's splendid achievement as the genius and assurance of the hereditary aristocrats who led them. On the field of Waterloo the great Duke gave his calm orders, and with equal calm and fortitude the rustics who manned the battered squares obeyed.

Of the 961,000 families engaged in agriculture in 1831, 686,000 were those of labourers who worked the land for others. The recent enclosures of the common lands had increased their numbers with many small-holders who, finding their hereditary tenures less valuable through loss of common rights or more onerous through heavy changes for enclosure or drainage, had disposed of them to their richer neighbours. In other ways the enclosures had operated against the interests of the labourer who, by legal processes little understood by him, had been deprived of certain prescriptive rights which had never had the formal recognition of law. As Arthur Young put it, 'The poor in these parishes may say, *Parliament may be tender of property; all I know is I had a cow, and an Act of Parliament has taken it from me.*' More often the cow was only a mangy donkey or a few straggling geese, but the right to keep them on the common and to gather firewood there had been an important item in a poor countryman's budget.

Yet if partially deprived, particularly in the southern counties, of his former and inadequately recognised stake in the land, robbed of his share in the dwindling wild food supply of the open countryside by cruel Game Laws and of a market for the products of his domestic handicrafts by the new machines, the peasant still clung to his hereditary standards and virtues. An intense confidence in his skill and capacity for work sustained him through a life of hardship—that and love of the land he tended. He was never so happy as when working regularly under a good master. Such men were neither the fantastic and passionate creatures of modern regional novelists nor the down-trodden puppets of sentimental social historians. Their intellects were naïvely elementary, their passions (as natural to those who worked hard on the soil) unobtrusive, their instinctive feelings profound. They conformed to the natural rhythm of life, and in this lay their enduring strength. Love of the soil, love of food—'bee-acon wi' fat about three inches thick, tha's the tackul!'—pride in their own strength and skill—'I 'eeant very big but I can carry a sack of whait ur wuts ur beeans wi' anybody'—and unshakable integrity and conservatism were the attributes of the English peasantry.

'Wurken on the land is lovely wurk', was the ungrudging verdict of an old Buckinghamshire labourer after a life of ceaseless labour, 'and in mi time I wurked furteen and fifteen hours a day, but that was afuur the machines come about. We sowed by hand, ripped by hand, and threshed wi' the thraiul. It was lovely wurk, and that was how it done when I was a young man. We used to dibble the sayd in, and I a' dibbled many a aiacre of wheeat, beeans, wuts and barley. Sometimes we used to sow bradcast. At harvist we cut wi' a sickle.' At times the same witness spoke in the language of poetry of his feeling for the land.

Some people think they can git summut out a nauthing—but they can't, and nivver wull. All me life I a noaticed that land wi' no dress gis very poour craps—short straa, little eeurs, and little kurnuls; but land well dressed always gis good craps—long straa, long eeurs, and big kurnuls: and I nivver yit sin big eeurs wi' fat kurnuls an thin short straa, and nobody else nivver did. When carn is sold by weight, ant it beeter to taiak a peck out a the sack, than put a peck in? That's the difference atween good and bad farmin'.

You must a cleean land, plenty a dress, and plenty a laiabour to git th' increeas and when ye a got these, the increeas comes.

Such a man when his time came to die could look round on an entire countryside which he had helped to cultivate.

A rough, simple, pastoral people, of great staying power, invincible good humour and delicate natural justice, such were the labourers of rural England. 'Here lies', runs a Gloucestershire epitaph

JOHN HIGGS
A famous man for killing pigs,
For killing pigs was his delight
Both morning, afternoon and night.

Set against the background of their industry, their homely pleasures assume an almost epic dignity. One loves to think of them in the taproom of the thatched ale-house in the evening over their modest pint of mild when their day's work was done—the high settles in the chimney corner, the bacon rack on the oaken beam, the sanded floor, the old brightly worn furniture gleaming in the flickering firelight.

Higher in the economic scale than the labourer was the smallholder. He still represented a substantial element in the rural community. With the village craftsman—a numerous class—he constituted the social and moral backbone of the parish. In 1831 one countryman in three possessed a stake in the land. One in seven worked his own land without hiring labour. Such a man—often a yeoman who held his tenure for life—was still the standard rustic Englishman.

The old cottage-folk of England were very tenacious of the good things of life they had been brought up by their fathers to honour. They liked to keep a bright fire burning on the hearth, choice old china on spotless shelves, smoked flitches of bacon and ham hanging from the ceiling, and home-brewed wine to offer their neighbours. They took pride in their mastery of oven and vat: in their skill in keeping garden: in raising poultry and bees. Above all they valued the virtues of decent living and good neighbourhood—honesty, truth, and purity of word and life.

Though the process was a more gradual one than has been generally realised, the yeoman type was slowly disappearing. It was too conservative to compete successfully with the more ruthless and greedier values set by urban and industrial commerce. And the tendency of landlords was to allow the old tenures for life—a rustic economy based not on accountant's statistics but on the rhythm of the human heart and body—to expire when they fell in. In their place they offered annual or determinable leases. The number of lifehold properties and copyholds of inheritance was therefore every year diminishing.

The older, smaller type of squire was also departing—killed by the violent fluctuations which followed in the wake of the Napoleonic wars and by the rising standard of social expense set by rich neighbours. But he was still to be found in considerable numbers in the remoter parts of the country—particularly in Devonshire, Wales, and Clun Forest, in the Fens and in the Yorkshire and Cumberland dales. Like the old hero of Scawen Blunt's poem he liked the hunting of the hare better than that of the fox, spoke in dialect, dined at six, and spent his evening over a long pipe and a tankard in the village inn. The pride of his house was the gun-room which he called his hunting parlour. In

white breeches and buckled shoes, fawn-coloured
leathers, tight double-breasted, brass-buttoned, bright
blue coat, buff vest, and low top hat—for he inclined to
the 'old Anglesey school of dressers'—he was still an
essential part of the English landscape.

To him and his kind, defying the sombre black of the
encroaching towns, that landscape owed at least a part
of its enchantment. He supplied it with pageantry. The
lovely primary colours of the English past that today
survive only in the dress uniform of the Guards and the
huntsman's coat shone in front of the vivid greenery of
May or glowed through the mists of autumn. So, too,
long afterwards when England had grown drab and
urban, old men recalled with a thrill of pleasure the
sight of the mail coaches, thirty or forty a day in any
fair-sized main-road town: 'the dashing steeds, the
fanfaronades on the horn, the scarlet coats of the
coachmen and the guard.'

Down by the coasts the country looked out on the sea.
In white Jane Austen houses along the Solent one could
see through the vistas in the trees the great battleships
with their bellying sails and the stately West Indiamen
'sailing between worlds and worlds with steady wing.'
Here was the watery highway from which the new
England drew its ever-expanding wealth, with clippers
bringing tribute from Pagoda Bay and the far ends of
the earth, and the rough, passionate sailors whom
coastwise England bred, singing as they pulled on the
ropes how soon they would

> . . . be in London city,
> Blow my bully boys blow!
> And see the girls all dressed so pretty,
> Blow! boys, blow!

Such men, by modern standards, lived lives of almost indescribable hardship, spending years afloat before they set foot on shore and, cleaned out by a single gargantuan and open-handed debauch, signing on again a few days later for another voyage. They were ready, like their fathers who fought under Nelson, to dare and do almost anything, and the safety and wealth of England rested on their rude, unconscious shoulders. For them the great shipbuilding yards on the Thames still turned out wooden ships of a quality unmatched throughout the world, made by men who had learnt their craft—part of England's hereditary wealth—from their forbears. 'His father's name before him was Chips, and his father's name before him was Chips, and they were all Chipses.'

Pride in craftsmanship and skill handed down the generations were the attributes which made the products of English manufacture sought and honoured throughout the earth. Their hallmark was quality, and they bore the unmistakable stamp of a nation of aristocrats. In the Lancashire cotton mills and the London slums a proletarian labouring class was fast emerging, but its significance was still hidden from contemporaries by the multitude of skilled craftsmen who constituted the rank and file of British industry. Except for cotton, no textile trade had been radically affected by machinery before 1830; wool-combing was still governed by skill of hand as was the hardware industry of the Midlands and the cutlery of Sheffield. The old trades were still more extensive than the new: at the time of the Reform Bill, there were more shoemakers in England than coal-miners. The unit of industry was very small: apprentices frequently lived with their employers over their own workshop, and every craftsman might aspire to be a master. The Spitalfields weavers of London, who on summer evenings could be seen seated in the porticos of their houses enjoying their pipes or digging their allotments in Saunderson's Gardens, the two hundred thousand bricklayers, masons, carpenters, house-painters, slaters, plumbers, plasterers, and glaziers who made up the close corporation of the building trade, the serge and cloth workers of the West Country, Gloucestershire, and East Anglia, the bootmakers of Northampton, the blanketers of Whitney, the chair-turners of the southern Chilterns, and the cabinet-makers and clock-makers of almost every county town were—for all the threat of the new machines to their employment and standards of living—men with a status in the country based on personal skill and character.

So were the rural handicraftsmen—blacksmiths, wheelwrights, carpenters, millers, cobblers—the fishermen and sailors of the coast towns and the engineers who were coming into existence to make and tend the new machines of steel and iron. North of the border in Lanarkshire, a French traveller found the Scottish craftsmen the best educated in Europe, 'well-informed, appreciating with sagacity the practice of their trade and judging rationally of the power of their tools and the efficiency of their machinery.' Such men—even the Durham miners whose working conditions so distressed Cobbett—enjoyed solid houses, substantial fare, and fine sturdy furniture made by craftsmen worthy of themselves. Pride in their domestic establishment was the hallmark of the British artisan and his wife: the Handloom Weavers' Commissioners' Reports of 1838 speak of the Midland weavers' cottages as good and comfortable and much superior to those of the surrounding agricultural labourers, with a solid dower of nice clocks, beds, and drawers and ornamented with prints. Within was cleanliness, good order, and fine frugal cooking.

Such was the old English system. It was based on the home, and home spelt contentment. Here was the seat of man's love—of his birth and his continuance. Here, too, he did his work. For the cottage, so long as the old economy persisted, was often both home and factory. Yarn was spun and woven under a single roof: 'the wife and daughter spun the yarn and the father wove.' Cottage labour for the womenfolk, such as the beautiful lace industry of old Buckinghamshire, supplemented the household income and gave an additional pride and interest to family life. In his leisure hours the good man, home from farm or smithy, cultivated his own little piece of land. 'He was no proletarian, he had a stake in the country, he was permanently settled and stood one step higher in society than the English workman of to-day.' Such men, as Engels wrote in the changing world of 1844, 'did not need to overwork; they did no more than they chose to do, and yet earned what they needed.'

They were rooted fast in their own soil. They had faith, they had home, and they had love. They were freemen, for within their narrow bounds they had freedom of choice. 'But intellectually, they were dead; lived only for their petty private interest, for their looms and gardens, and knew nothing of the mighty movement which, beyond their horizon, was sweeping through mankind. They were comfortable in their silent vegetation and but for the industrial revolution they would never have emerged from this existence, which, cosily romantic as it was, was nevertheless not worthy of human beings.' For to the pure but rootless intellect of the German radical, Engels, they did not seem human beings.

For those who were fortunate enough to inherit a share in that vanished rural England—for all not imprisoned in the great industrial towns or disinherited by the poverty which followed the enclosures—there was a sober joy in it. It came from healthy living, from quietude begotten of continuity, from the perceiving eye and the undulled sense. In the letters of Edward Fitzgerald one sees green England sunning herself in her immemorial peace—'the same level meadow with geese upon it . . . the same pollard oaks, with now and then the butcher or the washerwomen trundling by in their carts.' 'I read of mornings the same old books over and over again,' he writes, 'walk with my great dog of an afternoon and at evening sit with open window, up to which China roses climb, with my pipe while the blackbirds and thrushes begin to rustle bedwards in the garden.' 'We have had,' he wrote on another occasion, 'glorious weather, new pease and young potatoes, fresh milk (how good!) and a cool library to sit in of mornings.' Down in his native Suffolk this gentle pariot found the heart of England beating healthily: whenever he returned from sophisticated London he was amazed at 'the humour and worth and noble feeling in the country.' Fishing in 'the land of old Bunyan . . . and the perennial Ouse, making many a fantastic winding . . . to fertilize and adorn,' he stayed at an inn, 'the cleanest, the sweetest, the civillest, the quietest, the liveliest and the cheapest that was ever built or conducted . . . On one side it has a garden, then the meadows through which winds the Ouse: on the other the public road, with its coaches hurrying on to London, its market people halting to drink, its farmers, horsemen and foot travellers. So, as one's humour is, one can have whichever phase of life one pleases: quietude or bustle; solitude or the busy hum of men: one can sit in the principal room with a tankard and a pipe and see both these phases at once through the windows that open upon either.'

To such a one the changing seasons only brought new contentment—spring 'Tacitus lying at full length on a bench in the garden, a nightingale singing and some red anemones eyeing the sun manfully,' and autumn 'howling winds and pelting rains and leaves already turned yellow' with a book before a great fire in the evening. 'In this big London,' Fitzgerald wrote to Bernard Barton, 'all full of intellect and pleasure and business, I feel pleasure in dipping down into the country and rubbing my hand over the cool dew upon the pastures, as it were . . . I should like to live in a small house just outside a pleasant English town all the days of my life, making myself useful in a humble way, reading my books and playing a rubber of whist at night. But England cannot expect long such a reign of inward quiet as to suffer men to dwell so easily to themselves.'

For he knew that it could not last. The portents of change were already blazing in the northern and midland sky.

The sun shines very bright, and there is a kind of bustle in these clean streets, because there is to be a grand True Blue dinner in the Town Hall. Not that I am going: in an hour or two I shall be out in the fields rambling alone. I read *Burnet's History—ex pede Herculem*. Well, say as you will, there is not, and never was, such a country as old England—never were there such a gentry as the English. They will be the distinguishing mark and glory of England in history, as the arts were of Greece, and war of Rome. I am sure no travel would carry me to any land so beautiful as the good sense, justice, and liberality of my good countrymen make this. And I cling the closer to it, because I feel that we are going down the hill, and shall perhaps live ourselves to talk of all this independence as a thing that has been.

Our Past Proclaims our Future

ONE HUNDRED YEARS AGO, in the hey day of Britain's naval, commercial, and colonial ascendancy, the poet Swinburne wrote of her:

> All our past acclaims our future: Shakespeare's
> voice and Nelson's hand,
> Milton's faith and Wordsworth's trust in this our
> chosen and chainless land,
> Bear us witness: come the world against her,
> England yet shall stand.

Is it still true in the very different circumstances in which England, and the British people, find themselves today? And is it true what William Pitt declared a century earlier, when Britain stood alone, facing across the narrow seas a revolutionary nation in arms with three times her population, and with all western Europe aligned against her, with her own industrial districts starving, Ireland in rebellion and even the Fleet in mutiny—'I am not afraid for England. We shall stand till the day of judgement.'

To answer that question, one must first ask what England—or Britain—is? And I, who am no prophet, politician, or social reformer, can only answer it as a historian. Our past made us, made us a nation, gave us as a people a unity without which no people can become or remain a nation. The psalmist defined the truth of that necessity in the translated words of our lovely and inspired English liturgy: 'O pray for the peace of Jerusalem; they shall prosper that love thee. Peace be within thy walls and plenteousness within thy palaces. For my brethren and companions' sakes I will wish thee prosperity.'

We must go back to the past to find an answer. Only forty years ago, when the fate of the whole world and of Christian civilisation depended on our national unity, faced by a supreme crisis we proved beyond doubt a united people, a single nation. And forty years is a very small period in the history of a nation evolved in the course of fifteen centuries. Historically speaking, whatever we were in 1940, we still, substantially, must be. How did we come to be what we were and, as I believe, despite all we have since passed through, still are?

Our history is the history of the people of a northern island, moored off the western shores of the great continental land-bloc of Europe and Asia. All its original inhabitants came here by sea and were, therefore, seafarers; all of them learnt, as a result of bitter struggle and difficulty, to live with, intermingle with, and tolerate, one another. Seafaring, adventure, resilience, and dogged endurance in the face of difficulties was in their mixed—very mixed—blood; characteristics strengthened over the centuries by the vicissitudes of an island climate—a climate which, because of its ocean changeability, tended to make those who farmed and lived subject to its vagaries, adaptable and resourceful, though distrustful and chary of long-term planning and of anything too logical and rigid for this uncertain world.

In the course of centuries those who had made the island their home—the descendants of those first savage invaders—learnt not only to adapt themselves to, and live in comparative peace with, the others, but also to encompass the narrow seas round Britain—so vulnerable to invasion from the neighbouring continental heartland—with a strong fleet. This served, as Shakespeare put it, in the office of a wall or moat 'against infection and the hand of war', and made Britain an island not only geographically but also strategically. 'Britannia needs no bulwarks', wrote a later poet, when the greatest of all Europe's military conquerors was waiting on the other side of the Channel to invade us,

> No towers along the steep.
> Her march is o'er the ocean waves,
> Her home is on the deep.

This age-long security by sea has allowed to our system of government a greater measure of liberty and political diversity, of freedom of action, debate, and expression, than is easily possible in less happily situated and circumstanced lands where the menace of foreign invasion makes authoritarian government—swift and immediate, though tyrannical—an often unavoidable preservative of a nation's safety.

The most important of all the many invaders of our island, and those who had the greatest influence on our history, were the handful who came, not like the fierce Celts, Saxons, Danes, and Normans, with long-boat, fire and sword, but who arrived on our shores armed only with a cross, and the faith and courage which that cross gave.

I saw them march from Dover, long ago,
With a silver cross before them singing low,
Monks of Rome, from their home, where
   the blue seas break in foam,
Augustine with his feet of snow.

Others like them came from St. Patrick's Ireland and St. Columbia's Iona to convert the fierce northern warriors and clansmen of Northumbria and Caledonia to Christ's gentle creed of love and sacrifice, and to the revolutionary belief, inherent in Christianity, that every individual is a potential soul of equal value in the eyes of God, with a right to be respected and to live his life in his own way. It is this belief in the sanctity of the individual, and of the Christian creed and ethic, which has shaped the ideals of the English—and British—and, with them, by and large, their history. Obstinate, self-opinionated, and self-righteous, as are all peoples, and often as individuals, aggressive, quarrelsome, and greedy, yet in their corporate capacity returning again and again to the inner beliefs of a Christian nation.

For England is a Christian land, and only by contemplation of her long Christian history can one comprehend her. Her cathedrals and parish churches mark the milestones of her passage through time. Her civilisation was made by them, grew out of the arts, learning, and creed which those who raised and tended them taught, and if they crumble or are destroyed, must perish with them. Their aisles and towers have witnessed our whole history as a nation; were there when the news of Crécy and Agincourt, the defeat of the Armada, and the deliverance of the Nile and Trafalgar set their bells ringing; and through all the peaceful years of springtide, summer's suns, harvest, and winter's snows, have been the centre and inspiration of all the great moments of ordinary men's and women's lives. They knit us together as a people, like the Abbey at Westminster 'make us we'; without them ours would be a raw materialistic polity of concrete factories and offices and purposeless urban populations fast receding into barbarism. Lincoln, towering in shafts of light above the city, Canterbury's 'Bell Harry' and glorious nave enshrining the earliest home of English Christianity and the grave of the 'holy blissful martyr' who died to ensure the Church should never be the mouthpiece of a soulless State: York, Gloucester, Salisbury, Chichester, and Winchester, where Jane Austen's ashes rest under the feet of passing worshippers and sightseers; it is these and all the thousands of churches like them in every corner of the land which link us to those who have gone before and give meaning and purpose to our lives as members of a continuing nation.

> By altars old their banners fade
> Beneath dear spires; their names are set
> In minster aisle, in yew tree shade;
> Their memories fight for England yet.

There has been a further influence on our history which has helped to shape our destinies, institutions, and habits of thought, and given us, as a nation, unity and direction—the monarchy. This, too, is part of our Christian heritage, for the essence and justification of our hereditary monarchy is, and always has been, that it is a Christian monarchy. Its true founder was King Alfred of Wessex—one of the greatest men who ever lived and a direct ancestor of our present Queen and of all her predecessors of the House of Windsor. Having, by his leadership, saved Wessex and all England from the fierce pagan Norsemen who were then ravaging and on the point of destroying western Christendom, in his hour of victory this noble and heroic leader practised the greatest of Christian virtues. By offering his cruel foes baptism and forgiveness, he made it possible for Danes and Englishmen to live together in a single island and share a common Christian civilisation. No greater act of statesmanship was ever performed by an English ruler. And in the intervals of rebuilding his broken realm, he undertook the task—as heroic as any of his feats in battle—of translating single-handed the works of Christian lore and learning which alone could impart to his rude people the wisdom and faith he wished them to share. It was the deeply sincere attempt of this wise and humble warrior to model his life and his reign on that of his Master which made his achievement so memorable. He not only saved his kingdom but made it worth saving. His legacy to his country was his conception and example of what a Christian king should be—an ideal of monarchy which was not of vainglory but of Christian service.

Alfred's great-nephew, Edgar, was the first acknowledged King of all England. It was at his coronation in Bath Abbey in 973 that the earliest form of the Coronation Service still used at the crowning of England's kings was observed. Behind its solemn rites—the royal prostration and oath, the consecration and anointing, the anthem, 'Zadok the Priest', linking the kings of the Anglo-Saxons with those of the ancient Hebrews, the investiture with sword, sceptre, and rod of justice—lay the idea that an anointed king and his people were a partnership under God. After that sacramental act, loyalty to the Crown became a

Christian obligation. The ideal of patriotism, centering round the Crown, began to take shape in men's minds, superseding the older conceptions of tribal king and chieftain.

Ever since the days of that far crowning, the monarchy has served to implant in men's minds the habit of feeling and acting together in national matters. For a thousand years the Crown has been the key to England's—and, since the union of the Scottish and English crowns, Britain's—nationhood. Under the aegis of the hereditary monarchy it became natural to Englishmen, and even Anglo-Norman barons, to act with and through the Crown. For the functioning of their local institutions, the inheritance of their lands, the administration of justice and order, were all inextricably bound up with its existence. As every-where in the Middle Ages, society in England was intensely local; men lived and thought in terms of neighbourhood. Yet, as a result of three and a half centuries of evolution, her political and legal organisa-tion became, not provincial like that of medieval France, Spain, Germany, and Italy, but monarchical. The Crown was the motive-spark of public activity and the fount of honour. An English landowner thought of himself not merely as the vassal of the provincial earl, but as a liege of the King; and an English justice not as a functionary of a provincial court, but as a guardian of the King's peace. The organisation of the realm ceased to be feudal as on the continent; it became national. From top to bottom ran this chain of royal unity. The great men who ruled the provinces were also officers of the Sovereign's household, judicial bench, and feudal array. They governed the neighbourhood and they served the King. In a descending scale the same principle applied to every division of the nation; to those who operated its institutions in shire, hundred, and village, the baronial honour and manor. All stood, in one capacity or another, on the rungs of a ladder, feudal or administrative, which stretched upwards to the Throne.

England was very fortunate that during the first three centuries after the Norman conquest so many of her rulers possessed kingly qualities. Of those early Kings who by their strong rule gave England unity, the most original and far-reaching in achievement was the first Plantagenet, Henry II. The field in which this restless but marvellous creative genius mastered the feudal barons who, in the reign of his weak predecessor, had kept the country in perpetual turmoil, was not that of arms but of law. Through royal writs, traversing the anarchical power of the feudal jurisdictions, he achieved a major and peaceful revolution under the guise of restoring 'the good old laws'. Appealing to native English tradition, he used his prerogative to bring the whole system of freehold tenure under national law. By making the smaller landowner's right to his property dependent on the royal instead of feudal courts, he struck at the root of the great lord's power over his military tenants. And he dealt a death-blow to trial-by-battle and private war. Selfish, crafty, unscrupulous, the great lawyer-king wielded the sword of justice 'for the punishment of evil-doers and the maintenance of peace and quiet for honest men'. His judges made his remedies available in every corner of the realm. With the precedents they enshrined in their judgments, they created a Common Law for all England. They nationalised, as it were, the law.

By the end of Henry's reign there was no major offence against the public peace which could not bring the offender within range of a royal writ. All this prepared the way for the rule of law which was to become the dominant trait in England's life. Henceforward, whoever gave law to her was to have a machinery by which it could be enforced—against the strong as well as the weak. The professional judges Henry trained, the regular courts in which they sat, the writs they devised to meet popular needs and the judgments they left behind to guide their successors, helped to ensure that justice should be done even in the royal absence or in the reign of a weak or unjust sovereign. By making the Common Law the permanent embodiment of a righteous king sitting in judgement, the great Angevin established the English habit of obedience to law which has been the strongest of all the forces making for the nation's peaceful continuity and progress.

One great Plantagenet King established a Common Law for all England; another, his great-grandson, Edward I, a constitutional means, Parliament, for securing his people's consent to changing the law. Before his time, when the King wished to take counsel with the nation's most powerful men—or when he wished to obtain additional money from them, other than the permanent feudal and traditional dues—he called his magnates together in his Magnum Concilium or Great Council. During the struggles between them and Henry II's son and grandson, John and Henry III, the Great Council acquired what was more or less a right to be consulted at not too distant intervals. That it should be so was one of the provisions, though by no means always observed, of Magna Carta; that whenever he sought to depart from the established custom or 'known law of the land', the King together with his officers of state, should take counsel with his tenants-in-chief. It was Edward I who laid down, as the cardinal principle of this rule, the dictum that that 'which touches all should be approved by all', that to govern England effectively there must be 'counsel and consent'. By using periodic royal Parliaments, as they came to be called, to change and state the law, Edward gave this institution the bent which was to make it, in the fullness of time, the sovereign body it now is. With its representatives drawn from the lesser landowners or knights of the shire and from the burgesses of the trading towns, as well as from the magnates and prelates, its powers developed, partly through the desire of strong rulers to secure the utmost effective popular support for their policies, partly through the subject's growing resolve to make bad rulers conform to law. Sovereigns like Edward I, Edward III, and Henry VIII used and fostered Parliament because they were natural leaders who believed in carrying their people with them and making them active partners in their projects. Weak and arbitrary sovereigns like Edward II, Richard II, and Charles I helped the advance of Parliament—or rather of that inherent partnership between Crown and Parliament which has been the key to English history—because, in uniting their people against them, they made Parliament the champion of popular rights and liberties. Great monarchs gave the country unity, and less successful ones, however unconsciously, fostered national self-government.

Three hundred years later, the tragic struggle between Crown and Parliament in the seventeenth century, when a new dynasty of Scottish Kings pedantically claimed a 'divine right' to overrule Parliament, caused a libertarian yet instinctively conservative, people to reconstitute its ancient monarchy on a more stable basis. This was that hereditary sovereigns should reign but not govern, leaving their responsibilities and odium to ministers responsible for their actions to Parliament and, though nominally appointed by the Crown, dependent on the confidence and support of the dominant party in the House of Commons. To that constitutional conception the present royal dynasty has remained unswervingly loyal during its two and half centuries on the throne—that is for more than a quarter of the English royal millennium. If, during that time, the political influence and prerogatives of the Crown have little by little diminished, its prestige and popularity have immeasurably increased. The British—a people with a genius for political evolution rather than revolution—have resuscitated an ancient and elsewhere largely discarded, institution and adapted it to the needs of a new age. Through their reluctance to change old names and forms, a conservative but essentially practical race hit on a political device which is not an anachronism, as it might seem to superficial observers, but a most effective means for preserving and strengthening a country's cohesion and stability. More perhaps than any other single factor, it has accounted for the astonishing steadiness and resilience of the nation during the present stormy century.

During the eighteenth and nineteenth centuries our ancestors made many mistakes, but they never, unlike us, forgot the lesson that our safety and our liberties depend on control of the sea. Not only our own liberties, but also those of others. Three times—against Napoleon, against Kaiser William's Germany, against Hitler —it enabled Britain to put a ring of salt water and desert round a tyrant-conqueror who had overrun Europe and hold him as in a cage till we and others were strong enough to enter that cage and throttle him. By so doing, we secured the continuance of that conception of political liberty and balance of power which has been the dominating principle for which we have stood throughout our history.

> The nations not so blest as thee
> Must in their turn to tyrants fall,
> But thou shalt flourish great and free,
> The pride and envy of them all.

So sang our eighteenth-century ancestors in their favourite song, *Rule, Britannia*, with its chorus,

> Rule, Britannia, Britannia rule the waves,
> Britons never never never shall be slaves.

which is not a boast, as it may sound, but merely a conditional clause: that so long as Britons take the trouble to rule the waves, they will never be slaves, but no longer. Our eighteenth and nineteenth century ancestors, like us, forgot many things, but they never forgot that and, for all their mistakes and follies, remained great and free. But *we* have forgotten it.

Today, in the long scale of our history, we seem to have thrown away, or partly thrown away, the sceptre of the seas—and of the air over the seas—and stand thereby in considerable peril. But thirty or forty years is a very short time in the history of a nation. And if we recover our ancient faith and spirit, those who think we are finished may receive, as others have received before them, a salutary surprise*

> Fight on, my men, says Sir Andrew Barton,
> I am hurt, but I am not slain,
> I'll lie me down and bleed a while
> And then rise up and fight again.
>
> Fight on my men, Sir Andrew saith,
> And never flinch before the foe,
> And stand ye fast by St. Andrew's cross
> Until ye hear my whistle blow.

The old Scots pirate dying on his quarter deck had the root of the matter in him. If the spirit of the nation can burn like his in adversity, all will be well with us or with our children and children's children, and as a nation we shall rise again and resume our ancient Miltonian precedence of teaching the nations how to live.

There is much that has failed our nation in the course of the past thirty or forty years. But one thing at least has not failed it—and that the most ancient of all our institutions: the Crown and the wearer of the Crown. In a little book, published some years ago, called *A Thousand Years of British Monarchy*, I wrote fifty thumb-nail sketches of our sovereigns from Edgar I— the first acknowledged King of all England who was crowned in Bath Abbey in 973—to the present Queen. I should like to quote from two of them:

> In 1819, shortly before his death, there was born to the Duke of Kent a daughter, christened Victoria, who, during the brief reigns of her two unprepossessing uncles, grew up—in the rural seclusion of Kensington Palace under the tutelage of her widowed mother—the

* Written before the Falklands crisis and 'Task Force South'.

one hope on which the continuance of the Hanoverian dynasty and the English Crown then seemed to depend. For at that time most progressive and liberal-minded men believed that hereditary monarchy was an irrational and obstructive anachronism, and that, following the example of the United States, Britain would soon be a republic.

The young princess who at the age of eighteen ascended the throne was to prove them wrong. On the day on which, arrayed in her nightgown, she learnt at 6 a.m. from the kneeling Archbishop of Canterbury and Lord Chamberlain that she was Queen, she wrote in her diary:

'Since it has pleased Providence to place me in this station I shall do my utmost to fulfil my duties towards my country. I am very young and perhaps in many, though not in all things, inexperienced, but I am sure that very few have more real good-will and more real desire to do what is fit and right than I have.'

For this young inheritor of an imperilled monarchical tradition, though no genius, was a woman of conscience and character. 'I will be good', she is reported to have said when first told of her future destiny.

Her sixty-four years' reign saw immense social and political changes. At its start the population of the British Isles was about 25 millions, and at its end more than 41 millions, and this despite the Irish Famine of 1846 and the mass emigration which halved the population of Ireland. The transformation of national wealth and habit was even greater; before the Queen died the British had become a predominantly urban and industrial people, dependent on ocean imports and manufactured exports, and no longer on their own fields.

Yet through all the immense changes of Victoria's reign, the national standards of honour, behaviour and self-help remained a constant factor, transcending differences of class, wealth, creed, and politics. They animated the cloth-capped Socialist and trade union agitator of the later years of the reign as much as the top-hatted Utilitarians of its earlier years. They were set largely by a court whose royal mistress represented her subjects' moral convictions and aspirations. The great Victorians—in statesmanship, science, industry, literature, philanthropy, exploration, and war—were as appropriately linked with the name of their Sovereign as the great Elizabethans had been with theirs.

So, in a sense, were the peoples of the vast multi-racial empire over which Victoria was Queen Empress, covering by the end of her reign nearly a quarter of the habitable globe and of its inhabitants. At her Diamond Jubilee in 1897, a vast military thanksgiving parade was held in London, with proud contingents drawn from every continent in the world. At the centre of that glittering procession, driving through dense, cheering crowds in an open carriage to St. Paul's, was the little old lady in black in whose name all this pageantry was enacted. 'From my heart', ran her message at the day's end, 'I thank my beloved people. May God bless them!'

Of George VI—who succeeded to the throne just forty years later, I wrote in the same book of miniature sketches of our royal rulers and their reigns:

George VI perfectly symbolised the endurance and courage of a sadly buffeted British generation. When he was eighteen and World War I broke out, he went to sea, serving at Jutland, the most important naval engagement since Trafalgar. Later he became one of the first officers of the new Fighting Service to which the 1914–18 War gave birth, the Royal Air Force.

In 1936, after serving his country with unassuming conscientiousness as Duke of York, he was unex-

pectedly called to the throne. Utterly distasteful as it
was to him to take a beloved brother's place, he showed
complete abnegation of self, accepting, with a dignity
which concealed a painful handicap of speech, the
interminable burdens and tasks of kingship. Two years
after he was crowned the storm of war again broke over
Europe. By 1940 the British people stood alone facing
the greatest menace of their history. Instinctively, they
looked to the Throne. They were not disappointed.
The King with his devoted consort and their children,
remained, resolute and imperturbable, at the post of
danger and duty. All Britons knew that under no
conceivable circumstances would their Sovereign—the
symbol of their courage and unity—falter or parley
with the foe. Like his Minister, Winston Churchill, he
embodied and stood for all the ancient, enduring
virtues of his country. By his steadiness he helped to
give the British people that unshakeable confidence
which astonished and ultimately restored a breaking
world. As the Stukas dived on his Palace, the clerks and
typists making their comfortless way to their daily
tasks amid scenes of desolation and destruction, and
the working folk who stood, bloody but unbowed,
among the ruins of their homes and household goods,
instinctively stiffened with pride. The King of England
was on the throne of his fathers; like the great
Elizabeth, he would not be by violence constrained.

Four years later, in June 1944, King George watched
the sailing of the great British–American armada which
was to liberate western Europe. It was the epitome of
his reign. This quiet, kindly courageous man and the
people he and his Queen so worthily represented had
withstood the worst that Fate could bring against
them, and, enduring all things in the confidence of the
righteousness of their cause, had prepared for four
years for this day, leaving no stone unturned that could
assure success. Those who, through their good nature
and trust in the intentions of others, had been so weak,

had made themselves strong, not because they admired or sought strength for its own sake, but because they had found that there was no other way by which they could defend and preserve their ideals.

In 1945, on VE Day and on VJ Day, the triumph of those ideals over both the Nazis and Japanese was consummated. On each of these occasions the people turned to the Throne, surrounding the Palace to acclaim their King and Queen. Many of the high, and perhaps foolish, hopes of that time of liberation and victory were falsified by later events. But though wickedness—tyranny, greed, intolerance and bad faith—as in other generations, survived the defeat of the wicked, the King's life, in peace as in war, continued to remind his subjects of the ideals for which they had fought and suffered. In his keeping, as in his father's, the Crown stood for the virtues which from age to age restrain the forces of evil—truth, gentleness, loving kindness, courage in affliction, strength in adversity, tenderness to the weak, constancy to pledged word and duty. Destined like his generation to inherit an iron age, King George passed through the fire unscathed and, in the crowded, terrible years of his short but momentous reign, never uttered a word or performed an act which was not worthy of the traditions of his country's ancient and Christian Throne.

When the Queen rode in state to the Jubilee Thanksgiving Service in St. Paul's Cathedral, we saw what the occupant of our ancient and Christian throne meant—and means—to her people. In those deeply moving moments when she made her way on foot through unfettered and rejoicing crowds from St. Paul's to the Guildhall—the love and trust that all feel for her found spontaneous expression. For in a century of change and checkered national fortunes, one institution has never failed—the Crown and its wearer. 'Our Monarchy',

Lord Hailsham has written 'is the one part of our Constitution which is still working as it was designed to do.' In her person, her unfailing devotion to duty, her quiet dignity and self-command, the Queen has represented all that is best and truest in the character of the British people.

The legal and spiritual association of men of different creeds, callings, and classes in a nation, though often taken for granted, is a more wonderful miracle of cumulative human effort and wisdom than even the greatest achievement of science. For it enables millions who have never set eyes on one another to act together in peace and mutual trust. There can be no truer service than to preserve such a union, and prevent those millions from dissolving into antagonistic and destructive groups. In Britain it is the monarchy, though long divested of political responsibility, which reminds men that the political and economic differences which divide them are less real than the ties of history and common service which unite them.

The Queen does not only symbolise and help to promote, the unity of her people, she serves to remind them of their ideals. She represents in her person and family life, and in her dedication to her public duties, the abiding virtues of hearth, home, and service on the foundations of which society rests. She brings, in Burke's phrase, 'the dispositions that are lovely in private life into the service and conduct of the commonwealth.' In that transfigured moment during her Coronation—witnessed not only by the vast congregation in the Abbey but, through the miracle of television, by millions of her subjects throughout the world—she was bidden in God's name to 'do justice, stop the growth of iniquity, protect the Holy Church of God, help and defend widows and orphans, restore the things that are gone to decay, maintain the things that are restored, punish and reform what is amiss and confirm what is in good order.' By the example set from the throne, by the sincerity of her self-dedication to her unique and lonely task of serving her subjects all the days of her life, the Queen is the guarantee under God that those who direct the destinies of the nation will endeavour in her name to do those things.